Israel and Palestine

Bernard Wasserstein was born in London in 1948 and educated at Oxford and at the Hebrew University of Jerusalem. From 1980 to 1996 he was a member of the History Department at Brandeis University in Massachusetts and from 1996 to 2000 served as President of the Oxford Centre for Hebrew and Jewish Studies. He is now Professor of History at the University of Glasgow and is currently a visiting Fellow at the National Humanities Center in North Carolina. His books, which have been translated into French, German, Dutch, Hebrew, Arabic and Romanian, include *Britain and the Jews of Europe 1939–1945* and *The Secret Lives of Trebitsch Lincoln* which received the Golden Dagger Prize for Non-fiction. *Vanishing Diaspora: The Jews in Europe since 1945* provoked impassioned debate with its forecast of the demise of European Jewry. His most recent book was *Divided Jerusalem*, also published by Profile Books.

Israel and Palestine

Why They Fight and Can They Stop?

Bernard Wasserstein

P
PROFILE BOOKS

First published in Great Britain in 2003 by
Profile Books Ltd
58A Hatton Garden
London EC1N 8LX
www.profilebooks.co.uk

1 3 5 7 9 10 8 6 4 2

Typeset in Lapidary 333 by MacGuru
info@macguru.org.uk

Printed and bound in Great Britain by
Clays, Bungay, Suffolk

A CIP catalogue record for this book is available from the British Library.

ISBN 1 86197 534 1

For Paulina

Contents

Acknowledgements

I am grateful to Balliol College, Oxford, for inviting me to deliver the Leonard Stein Lecture series for 2002 out of which this book grew. The lectureship was established in memory of the historian Leonard Stein, for whom, some thirty years ago, I had the privilege of working as a research assistant. I also wish to thank St Antony's College, Oxford, in whose Nissan Lecture Theatre the lectures were delivered. Julia Bray, Neil Caplan, Raymond Cohen, Menachem Klein, Ari Paltiel, Steve Pyne, Harriet Ritvo, Avi Shlaim, Helen Solterer, Kenneth W. Stein, and many others gave me information, advice and encouragement. Paulina Kewes and David Wasserstein read the entire manuscript and made helpful suggestions. The staffs of the Bodleian Library, Oxford, the University of Glasgow Library, the Central Zionist Archives, the Public Record Office, Kew, and the Israel State Archives afforded me access to their materials and a great deal of further assistance. The maps were drawn by Mike Shand of the University of Glasgow's Cartographic Unit. The graphs were prepared by Peter J. McKinney. I have benefited from generous support for my work from the University of Glasgow. This book was completed at the National Humanities Center in North Carolina, and I want to express particular gratitude to the Center and its staff for awarding me a fellowship there in 2002 and for providing admirable facilities for work, thought, and study. Finally, I wish to acknowledge my continuing debt to my publisher, Andrew Franklin, and to my editors, Penny Daniel and Trevor Horwood.

Jerusalem
January 2003

Figures

Maps

Introduction

Mon frère, mon semblable! Zionism and Palestinian nationalism, arising from different roots, drawing on profoundly different political cultures, and aiming at mutually antagonistic objectives, have strangely imitated each other down the decades. The mimicry may be observed in the thinking as well as in the behaviour of both movements. Each regards itself as the primary political expression of a victim nation and draws from that self-image a solipsistic self-righteousness that is used to justify ruthless means. Each has resorted to terrorism and offences against human rights. Each for long denied the national existence and legitimacy of the other. At the heart of each is an obsessive national vision, born of a century of war, and focused on population, land, work, security, and dignity. Each is now near the end of its tether.

Why do Israelis and Palestinians fight? Is their contest a zero-sum game that one side can win only at the price of totally obliterating the other? Many observers, horrified by the suffering of innocents and impatient for easy explanations, attribute the intractability of the conflict to supposedly immutable hatreds founded in ethnicity, religion, or culture. Others, quick to find convenient scapegoats, blame this or that individual or interested party for acting in allegedly criminal, irrational, dishonourable, or self-seeking ways. And some, striving to fit the history of the struggle into a larger conceptual framework, distort the contestants, their motives and objectives, as in a fairground mirror, into unrecognizable grotesques.

In this book I argue that there are sound and ascertainable reasons for the conflict. Israelis and Palestinians are not driven to kill one another by demons beyond human ken. The root of their quarrel is a matter neither of mutual misunderstanding nor of innate evil. Nor are the protagonists puppets in some larger global mime-play. The causes of their contention may be located in the particularities of their intertwined experiences over the past century. While some on both sides have been responsible for despicable acts of inhumanity, neither Jews nor Arabs, in their collective behaviour, are animated by crazed psychopathy. They fight over definable interests, motivated by comprehensible value-systems, in pursuit of identifiable goals.

I examine the history and contemporary reality of their struggle in four dimensions: demographic, socio-economic, environmental, and territorial. My purpose is to demonstrate that these facilitate more sober consideration of future possibilities than is provided by many backwards-facing accounts that focus on the familiar elements of ethnocentric nationalism, religious symbolism, diplomatic chicanery, and violence.

I should make clear that what I propose is not a reductionist interpretation but an attempt to redress the balance by bringing into the foreground some relatively neglected

1 People

'Demography', according to Auguste Comte, 'is destiny'. The linkage between political conflict and the population balance of contending groups is familiar to students of ethnic, religious, and other conflicts in many parts of the world. In Northern Ireland the slow erosion of the Protestant majority owing to the higher Catholic birth rate has been a significant aspect of the struggle between the two communities since the late 1960s. In the former USSR, the population growth of the non-Russian, especially the non-European, peoples – much more rapid than that of the dominant Russians – coloured the politics of the Soviet Empire increasingly in its final years and shaped the manner of its fall. In Lebanon, where the political system between 1943 and 1975 was based on allocation of government positions according to the supposed balance of the different religious groups in the population, it proved impossible to hold a census lest the delicate political status quo be upset by evidence of changed demographic realities; in the end, the extent of change, and in particular the decline in the Christian proportion of the population, overwhelmed the system anyway and, after a bitter fifteen-year-long civil war, a new dispensation emerged in which the Christians' political power was diminished.

The demographic imperative at the heart of the Israeli–Palestinian conflict is essential to its understanding. In 1900 Palestine had a population of not much more than half a million. By 2000 nearly ten million people lived in the area between the Mediterranean and the River Jordan. That twenty-fold multiplication in the course of the century constitutes one of the highest rates of growth of any country in the world.

The transformation was not merely in size but also in composition of population. In 1900 Palestine, part of the Muslim-dominated Ottoman Turkish Empire, was overwhelmingly Muslim: only around a fifth of the population was non-Muslim, roughly 10 per cent Christian and 10 per cent Jewish. By 2000 Christians formed only a tiny part of the population and Jews formed an absolute majority – a preponderance reflected in their political dominance in the country, and direct sovereignty over the greater part of it. One reason for the huge change in absolute population size was an unusually high rate of natural increase, particularly of the Muslim Arabs. But the primary reason for the change in population composition was mass immigration of Jews.

Jews – but not necessarily, in what initially impelled them towards Palestine, Zionists. Indeed, over the entire period of modern Jewish immigration since 1881, only a small minority of the immigrants were Zionists in their home countries. During the period of British rule in Palestine between 1917 and 1948, as later in the state of Israel, Jewish immigration was not, in the main, motivated by ideological commitment to Zionism – though it was often portrayed as such both by Zionists and by their enemies. Like all migratory movements, this was a mixture of repulsion from the old country and attraction to the new. But if we survey the successive waves of *aliya* (Jewish immigration to Palestine), it is plain that in the great majority of cases push was much more important than pull. Only a minority of Jewish immigrants had been active members of the Zionist movement before they arrived in Palestine/Israel. Most, in fact, went there only because other countries were closed to them.

This was certainly true of most of the German and central European Jews who fled to Palestine in the period after Hitler's ascent to power in 1933. Before Nazism, German Zionism had been one of the weaker territorial units of the movement and Zionists had constituted a small minority of German Jewry. Similarly in the case of the overwhelming mass of Jews expelled from Arab countries after the establishment of Israel in 1948. Notwithstanding attempts in Israel in recent years to create, as it were, a Zionist pedigree for the oriental Jewish communities, most Jews in Arab lands were hostile or at best lukewarm towards Zionism until force of circumstances dictated otherwise. So too were the million or more Jews who arrived in Israel from the USSR/CIS after 1988. Most of these, unlike the more ideologically inspired, and very much smaller, wave of Russian Jewish immigration between 1971 and 1979, were economic migrants. It is not widely known that in the case of Jewish migrants from Russia to Israel, the two main alternative (and often preferred) destinations, the USA and

Germany, have for several years enforced a numerical quota on admissions, thus, in effect, diverting the flow of emigration towards Israel.

Nevertheless, even if the greater part of Jewish immigration to Palestine and later to Israel was not motivated by Zionist conviction, most of the arrivals reinvented themselves as Zionists once they got there. In a common pattern of nationalist myth-making, they invested their (and their ancestors') presence in the country with a retrospective significance that was at variance with historical reality.

In recent years another historical myth has grown up to the effect that the chief source of population growth in modern Palestine was not natural increase but immigration, Arab no less than Jewish. The proposition has its origins in the work of serious economic and social historians who drew particular attention to the social and economic backwardness of Palestine before the start of modern Jewish immigration there in the 1880s and stressed that in that period Palestine had been largely barren and under-populated.[1] The argument was taken up by propagandists and exaggerated to absurd lengths. A best-selling book by Joan Peters, published in 1984, claimed that Jews outnumbered Muslims in Palestine in the late nineteenth century and that Jewish immigration between the 1880s and 1948 had been paralleled and even exceeded by massive, unrecorded Arab immigration from surrounding Arab lands. Peters went so far as to construct a conspiracy theory according to which British government officials in Palestine, between the end of the First World War and 1948, deliberately concealed this Arab influx while severely restricting immigration of Jews.[2] The hypothesis, a crude distortion of reality, based on misuse of historical documentation and misreading of census data, was easily demolished by professional historians.[3] Yet it came to enjoy an extended afterlife in the tenebrous borderland between historical scholarship and politics.

The true contours of the demography of late-Ottoman Palestine were very different. While impossible, given available data, to determine with total precision, the population of Palestine in the years before the First World War can be reliably estimated within reasonable margins of error. Unfortunately, Ottoman census figures are of limited value. Only Ottoman citizens were counted, thus excluding an important part of both the Jewish and, to a lesser extent, the Christian communities as well as, for other reasons, many of the nomadic Beduin and gipsy populations of Palestine's southern and eastern marches. We have a number of population estimates by foreign consuls and by Jewish investigators, but these are just that – estimates, whose value is sometimes vitiated by the special interests of those making them.

For a long time the figures assembled by Arthur Ruppin, the head of the Zionist Office in Jaffa between 1908 and 1914, were widely accepted. The German-born Ruppin, one of the founders of modern sociological study of the Jews, had acquired an intimate knowledge of the country and was a scrupulous and conscientious investigator. Using Ottoman government data as well as other sources of information, he calculated that there were 85,000 Jews in Palestine in 1914, constituting about 12 per cent of a total population of about 689,000, figures that were later treated respectfully by the British mandatory authorities. Ruppin's estimates as well as Peters's proposals, however, have recently been subjected to rigorous critical analysis by the Ottoman demographer Justin McCarthy. His calculation of the Jewish population in 1914, based on all the available evidence, is much smaller than Ruppin's: at most 60,000 – this out of a total population of 798,000.[4] McCarthy's methodology and his results have in turn been effectively challenged by the late U. O. Schmelz, who proposes a lower figure for the total population in 1914 and a higher one for the Jewish – essentially a return to the Ruppin estimates.[5]

The controversy is of more than technical interest. It forms part of the armoury of statistical data that Zionist and Arab nationalist political antagonists in the struggle for Palestine draw on as each attempts to prove that it is the more deeply rooted in the country. We should not be surprised, therefore, to find that McCarthy's work is published in a series of the Institute for Palestine Studies (an offshoot of the Palestine Liberation Organization). Nor that the former Israeli Prime Minister Binyamin Netanyahu commended Peters's book on his website and boasted to a meeting of his supporters of how he had floored a CNN interviewer by pointing out that until the start of the return of the Jews 'there wasn't a living soul here'.[6] In the absence of more precise data, Ruppin's figures, particularly for the Jewish population, may probably be accepted as closest to reality.

Given the smallness of the Jewish minority in Palestine in the late nineteenth century, there were few, even among the nationalist-minded settlers, mainly refugees from Russia and Romania after 1881, who dared to dream of a Jewish majority in the country. Hence the readiness of some Zionists, such as the Russo-Jewish writer and thinker Ahad Ha-am (Asher Ginzberg), to speak in terms of a spiritual rather than a political home in Palestine. Only after the foundation of the Zionist Organization by Theodor Herzl in 1897 did the prospect of a Jewish majority, to be attained by the systematic mobilization of mass immigration, begin to be seriously envisaged.

Zionist hopes of attaining demographic preponderance in Palestine, seen as an essential condition of political control, were given a boost by the Balfour Declaration of 1917, in which the British government undertook to facilitate the establishment of a Jewish National Home in Palestine, 'it being clearly understood that nothing shall be done which may prejudice the civil and religious rights of existing non-Jewish communities in Palestine or the rights and political status enjoyed by Jews in any other country'.[7] At the Paris Peace Conference in 1919, the Zionist leader, Chaim Weizmann, spoke of bringing in as many as seventy or eighty thousand Jews a year. The aim was to create a Jewish society of four or five million Jews that would form an overwhelming majority of the population. Weizmann's ambitious plans were initially supported by Winston Churchill – who, as Colonial Secretary in 1921–2, played a vital role in establishing the basis of British policy in the country – and by the first British High

Commissioner (head of the administration), Sir Herbert Samuel, who ruled Palestine from 1920 to 1925. In private correspondence, at the outset of his term of office, he looked forward in the long term to a Jewish majority and a Jewish government of the country:

> What is practicable now is one thing. What the present measures will lead to – and are designed to lead to in the future – is another. For the time being there will be no Jewish state, there will be restricted immigration; there will be cautious colonisation. In five years the pace will probably be accelerated and will grow after that progressively in speed. In fifty years there may be a Jewish majority in the population. Then the Government will be predominantly Jewish, and in the generation after that there may be that which might properly be called a Jewish country with a Jewish state. It is that prospect which rightly evokes such a fine enthusiasm, and it is the hope of realising that future which makes me ready to sacrifice much in the present.[8]

The Jewish National Home, established under British imperial protection between 1920 and 1948, could thus count, at any rate at the moment of its creation, on strong support for its central aim – the attainment of sovereignty by means of controlled immigration leading to a Jewish majority.

If Weizmann's targets had been achieved, the Jews would have attained majority status within a decade. Nor was Samuel behindhand in facilitating such an influx. The first immigration schedule set by the British mandatory government at its initiation in 1920 provided for 16,500 certificates to be issued in the first year: each certificate was for one breadwinner so that as many as 70,000 immigrants might have arrived. But as Moshe Mossek has shown, the Zionists found that, given their limited resources, they could afford to bring in only a small fraction of the numbers they had forecast. As early as October 1920 they asked for the schedule to be reduced to a mere 1,000. Henceforth they found themselves compelled by economic necessity to adopt a policy of strictly selective immigration.[9] Samuel was dissatisfied and complained to Weizmann: 'It would be a mistake to attempt to limit the number of Jewish immigrants in the near future to so small a figure as 1,000. There will be a very considerable demand for labour here.'[10] Embarrassed by their inability to realize their heady initial plans, the Zionists found it politically convenient to cast the responsibility for their own failure on the British administration – an interpretation that many historians happily embraced until recently. In 1922 the British introduced the criterion of 'economic absorptive capacity' as the governing principle affecting permitted levels of Jewish immigration; however, the chief constraint on the Jewish influx, at least until 1933, was not British policy but the inability of the Zionists to generate the large amounts of capital required to provide an economic base for the Jewish National Home.

In the mid-1920s the Zionists' selective immigration policy was briefly cast aside when a wave of petit bourgeois migrants from Poland, fleeing an economic crisis in their homeland, descended on Palestine. They travelled mainly under their own steam rather than as Zionist 'pioneers'. This *aliya* too arrived more as a result of push than of pull. Their choice of Palestine was largely a consequence of the coming into effect in 1924 of the Johnson Act in the United States, which abruptly foreclosed the possibility of their immigration to America. The sudden influx produced a short-lived boom, followed by a severe economic crisis and recession after 1927 that led to a short period of net emigration.

By 1929, as a result, instead of the Zionist majority foreshadowed by Weizmann's Peace Conference statement and by Samuel's initial immigration policy, a mere 100,000 Jewish immigrants had arrived, raising the number of Jews to 156,000, 16 per cent of the total population of the country. Zionist expectations for further progress had now been greatly scaled down. The Jewish Agency (the legal framework for Zionist activity in Palestine established under the mandate) calculated that, assuming current levels of natural increase and an average annual Jewish immigration of 15,000, the Jewish population would reach half a million by 1949. But by that time, the Arab population, merely as a result of natural increase, would be 1.1 million. The Jewish/Arab proportions would then be about 30/70. The head of the Jewish Agency's Political Department, Haim Arlosoroff, commented, 'If we shall be able to reach this mark within the next twenty years, it certainly will be all we could reasonably expect and hope for', though he added: 'As a matter of fact, in my view, such a ratio of numbers between the two groups in Palestine would render the actual predominance, economic, social and cultural, a settled matter – long before a statistical Jewish majority were reached.'[11] Arthur Ruppin, however, while broadly sharing Arlosoroff's view of the demographic prospects, pointed out it would most likely take another thirty or forty years after that before Jews could hope to attain a majority – and in the meantime it was doubtful whether the Jews would be able to continue to rely to such a degree on the help of the British administration.[12]

Shortly afterwards, the Great Depression began, hitting Zionist fund-raising in the Diaspora hard. By 1931 the Zionist enterprise appeared to be declining into insignificance, like so many earlier utopian settlement schemes. It was only the largely unplanned mass immigration of refugees from European anti-Semitism, especially in Germany and Poland, after 1932 that suddenly boosted the Jewish proportion of the population (see Figure 1).

Although the British mandatory government, unlike the Ottoman, produced relatively reliable population statistics, these too gave rise to controversy. The country's first modern census, conducted in 1922, yielded a total population of 757,000, of whom 84,000, or 11 per cent, were Jews (see Figure 2). This was a figure very disappointing to the Zionists, who had hoped to appear as a much larger element in the population. But the census was flawed, particularly in its figure for the Beduin of the Southern District. They refused to participate in the census, fearing, in the light of past experience,

Figure 1 **Jewish immigration to Palestine/Israel, 1919–2002**

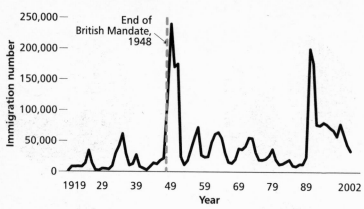

Note: For most years since 1948, figures include all persons admitted as immigrants under the Law of Return. Figure for 2002 is estimated.
Sources: *Encyclopaedia Judaica*; Israel Central Bureau of Statistics; *Statistical Handbook of Jewish Palestine 1947*; Israel Ministry of Immigration and Absorption.

that it might form a basis for military conscription and/or taxation. Their number in the census, as a result, was derived from what was described as 'information supplied by the principal sheikhs' and was given as 73,000 – a figure that was later conceded by the mandatory government to be greatly exaggerated. A more realistic estimate was said to be only 45,000.[13]

The best single source of information on the demography of Palestine under the British mandate is the two-volume report on the 1931 census. Unlike its predecessor, which was little more than a crude population count, this was a formidable scientific enterprise, a masterpiece of imperial ethnography, the basic principles and organization of which were inspired by Indian census laws.[14] It was conducted at a period

Figure 2 **Population of Mandatory Palestine/Israel by religious group, 1922–2000**

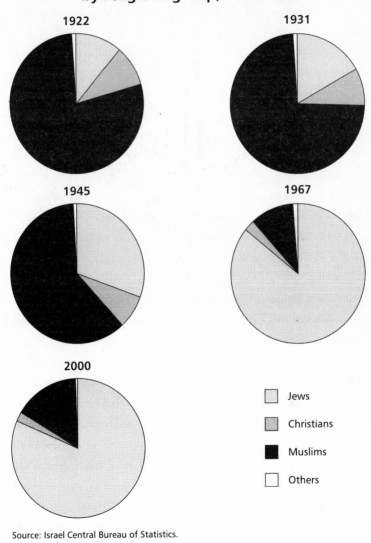

1922 1931

1945 1967

2000

Jews

Christians

Muslims

Others

Source: Israel Central Bureau of Statistics.

of simmering political tension in Palestine and the official records show how delicately the government had to tread in its arrangements, for fear of upsetting the susceptibilities of one or another section of the population.

In order to ensure compliance, the government decided to set up an unofficial advisory committee. But the Arab nationalist leaders insisted that they would participate only if they were represented on the committee in proportion to their existing share of the population, i.e. four Arabs to one Jew. The Jews lodged objections to this as well as setting conditions of their own on participation in a mixed committee. The government was therefore obliged to form two committees, one Jewish, the other Arab.[15] The director of the census, Eric Mills, a Colonial Service officer, was commended by the High Commissioner, Sir John Chancellor, for his skill in handling the committees, 'for their ingenuity and malevolence in imagining base motives which they impute to the government are hardly credible'.[16] The minutes of the proceedings of these committees bear out this jaundiced view.

The Arab Committee, for example, pressed that Palestinians resident abroad should be counted, bearing in mind the many who had emigrated to South America.[17] The obvious hope was thereby to boost the Arab count. The Arabs also demanded that the population should be differentiated on a national as well as a religious basis. In his lapidary report on the census, Mills noted:

> In fact the Jewish community is a 'nationality'.
> The consciousness of the existence of this

'nationality' has led the non-Jewish religious communities to a vague conception of an Arab 'nationality'. This Arab 'nationality' has no legal existence since there is no Arab community in any formal sense. Its basis is perhaps best described as an awareness on the part of some of the non-Jewish religious communities of the possibility of common factors in the aims of the several communities.

The Arabs demanded that the census should include a question enabling respondents to declare an Arab nationality and the government eventually decided that, as Mills put it, 'an opportunity should be given in the census to all persons to declare a "nationality" if they so desired'.[18]

The Jews, for their part, opposed the inclusion of any question regarding 'landlessness' or 'unemployment'.[19] Their fear was that such figures might lend substance to Arab complaints that Jewish land purchase was resulting in displacement of Arab peasants. Meanwhile, Vladimir Jabotinsky and his ultra-nationalist Revisionist Zionist movement called on the Jews to boycott the census on the ground that its object was 'to prove that the Jews are an insignificant minority' preparatory to the creation of a parliamentary government 'designed to stifle Zionism'.[20]

In the event, the census passed off with, by all accounts, full participation by the population – with the exception of the Beduin, whose numbers were once again estimated. This was intended to be the first of a series of quinquennial censuses. But the government's preoccupation with a large-scale Arab revolt between 1936 and 1939, followed by the war and then by the post-war Jewish revolt, precluded the holding of any further census before the end of the mandate. The 1931 census was therefore the only scientific census carried out in mandatory Palestine. Indeed, given the subsequent partition of the country, it is the only such census that has ever been carried out in a unified form covering the whole of the area west of the Jordan. For this reason, among others, it is the *locus classicus* for any serious discussion of the demography of Palestine under the mandate.

Among its most significant findings were the sets of data relating to birth and death rates. Following the census a further special inquiry was conducted in late 1931 on fertility patterns. These showed the extraordinary fecundity of the Palestinian population, particularly, though not only, the Muslims (see Figure 3). The birth rate for Palestinian Muslims in 1931, 53 per thousand, was much higher than that for Jews, 32 per thousand. But both were very high by contemporary international standards. Palestinian Muslims in this period had a higher gross reproduction rate than that of any country in the world. Even the Jewish rate in the period 1926–35 surpassed that for any European country except Romania and Portugal.[21] In a memorandum he prepared in 1934, Mills warmed to this theme, showing that the average number of children born alive to a Muslim family was over 8.5, to Christians 8, and Jews 6.7.[22] Population growth was somewhat reduced by high infant and child mortality: in 1938 the median age of Muslims in Palestine at death was

Figure 3   **Fertility rates by religion in Mandatory Palestine and Israel, 1926–2000**

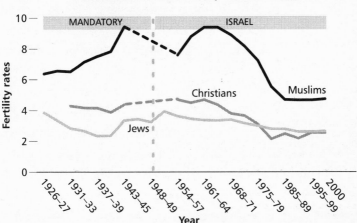

Sources: Roberto Bachi, *The Population of Israel* (Jerusalem, 1974); Israel Central Bureau of Statistics.

about two and the infant mortality rate was on a similar level to India. Jewish natural increase was able to keep pace with Arab natural increase to some degree because of the much lower Jewish infant mortality rate and also because of the lower Jewish death rate. Life expectancy at birth for Muslims in 1931 was forty-two, which was comparable to England and Wales in the 1870s, whereas for Palestinian Jews it was sixty, about the same as the UK in 1931.[23]

Against this background the Zionists and the Arabs engaged in anxious projection of rates of natural increase and their bearing on the future population balance of Palestine. The Zionists were particularly concerned from the late 1930s by accumulating evidence of a decline in Jewish

fertility as the Jewish population began the process of reduced rates of natural increase, already at that time apparent
in western European countries – the phenomenon that came
to be termed the 'demographic transition' and that in most
of Europe today has resulted in below-replacement rates of
natural population growth. This was one of the main reasons
for the Zionist tendency, in their selective immigration policy, to favour people of child-bearing age.

The government too engaged in such calculations, particularly after the outbreak of the Arab revolt. Following the ap-
pointment, in 1936, of a Royal Commission to inquire into
the Palestine problem, Mills prepared a graph projecting future population on the basis of existing rates of natural increase plus various levels of Jewish immigration. The result
(see Figure 4) showed that for the then Arab:Jewish population ratio of roughly 7:3 to be maintained, Jewish immigration would have to be restricted to 12,000 a year. That was,
in fact, the 'political high level', recommended by the Royal
Commission as a ceiling if the mandate were to continue in
its existing form. In late 1938 Mills was asked to recalculate
and came up with slightly revised figures, suggesting that immigration of about 15,000 per annum over the next few
years would be the relevant ceiling on the basis that the Jew-
ish:Arab population ratio was to be held steady.[24] Hence the
figure of 75,000 set in the government's White Paper of May
1939 as the limit on Jewish immigration over the next five
years – though one government official, J. S. Bennett, an en-
thusiast for preventing Jewish escape from Nazi Europe,
worried about 'the possibility (perhaps probability) of the

Figure 4   Palestine government projection of future population trends, 1937

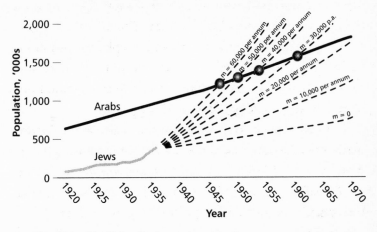

m = Annual rate of Jewish immigration.
Source: Palestine Royal Commission Report, 1937.

Jews temporarily relaxing birth-control in the face of numerical restriction [to immigration] and sending their numbers higher still'.[25] Mills's projections were largely borne out by the demographic developments of the next decade. The Jewish proportion rose only slightly, to about one-third of the total population of roughly two million at the end of the mandate.

The dramatic events of the Israeli War of Independence in 1947–9, of course, transformed the demographic balance. The displacement from their homes of most of the Arab population of what became Israel, followed by mass Jewish immigration of survivors of Hitler's Europe and Jewish refugees from Arab countries, brought the Jews much closer to their goal of an absolute majority. Within Israel only about 150,000 Arabs remained after the rest had fled or been expelled by Israeli forces. At least 700,000 refugees left, many proceeding beyond the borders of former mandatory Palestine to Transjordan, Syria, or Lebanon. But a large proportion remained in the Egyptian-occupied Gaza Strip and in the Cis-Jordanian region that came to be known as the West Bank. By 1952 Israel's Jewish population of 1.4 million surpassed the remaining Arab population in former mandatory Palestine of approximately 1.2 million.

In the course of the 1950s and early 1960s, Israeli leaders from time to time considered the hypothetical possibility of occupying the West Bank, particularly in the event of an overthrow of the Hashemite regime in Jordan. They were restrained in large measure by fear of the demographic consequences. The Israeli Prime Minister, Moshe Sharett, expressed the general view in 1954:

> Let us suppose that we conquer the rest of
> Palestine up to the Jordan River, I do not
> suppose that such a war would result in the same
> Arab exodus as during the previous one ... I am
> far from certain that our annexation of the West
> Bank inhabited by a million or so, would mean a
> marked improvement in our borders, in our
> ability to defend ourselves.

Alluding to the continuing external threat to Israel,

Sharett declared, 'I'm not sure which is preferable – an explosion from outside or from the inside.'[26]

When Israel occupied these regions in the course of her lightning victory in the 1967 war, a further exodus took place of about 200,000 from the West to the East Bank. The result was that at the end of 1967 about 1.2 million Arabs in the West Bank and Gaza remained under Israeli occupation. At that time Jews constituted two-thirds of the total population in the area under Israeli rule. By 1985 that ratio had narrowed to 63:37. The head of the Palestine Liberation Organization, Yasir Arafat, began to speak of a 'demographic bomb'. Sari Nusseibeh, a Jerusalem Arab intellectual and political moderate, added: 'Just making more babies is not enough … The demographic bomb will never explode without a fuse. The fuse will be our demand for equal rights.'[27] Those words were uttered in October 1987, a matter of weeks before the outbreak of the first Palestinian intifada.

In 2003 the Palestinian population of the West Bank and Gaza numbers about 3.3 million. Meanwhile the Arab population of Israel proper has increased to 1.3 million. Jews number about 5.1 million out of a total population in Israel and the occupied territories of around 10 million. Altogether the size of the Arab population of Palestine plus Israel today is rapidly approaching the Jewish and looks set to surpass it in the near future.

In recent years, as in earlier times, the primary engine of population growth has remained natural increase. This can be clearly illustrated by the fact that, in spite of massive Jewish immigration since 1988 of well over a million Jews from the former Soviet Union, the Arab proportion of the population within Israel has held its own and if anything increased. It has grown from 16 per cent in 1980 to 19 per cent today. The average number of children per woman among Israeli Jews has declined to about 2.5, still above population replacement level – but not by much. The equivalent figure for Israeli Arab women is 4.7. But although the natural increase rate of Israeli Arabs is higher than that of Israeli Jews, that of Palestinians in the occupied territories is even higher. As in the 1930s, the Palestinians are still one of the most fertile peoples on earth. Fewer than half of Palestinian women in the West Bank and Gaza use any form of modern contraceptive device. On average, they still have as many as six children each. Today their infant mortality and life expectancy levels have come close to convergence with those of Israeli Jews at near west-European levels. Therefore Israeli Jews depend critically on a continuing high level of immigration if they are to maintain the current rough parity in population, let alone improve their position.

But the flow of immigration to Israel has declined from the high levels of the early 1990s. The main reason is not the intifada but rather the fact that, with the virtual emptying-out of all Jewish communities of distress, apart from the 20,000 or so Jews remaining in Iran, the reservoir of potential future Jewish immigration to Israel has virtually dried up. Fewer than half a million Jews remain in the entire former Soviet Union – and migration to Israel has fallen off from the peak figures of the early 1990s.[28] The economic crisis in Argentina in 2002 brought a short-lived flurry of interest in *aliya* among the 235,000 Jews of that country. Substantial efforts were made by the Jewish Agency and the Israeli government to persuade them to move to Israel. In the event, most stayed put, at any rate for the time being; those who left headed mainly for North America or Spain rather than Israel.

Moreover, Israel, like all countries of immigration, is also a country of emigration. Family, educational and other overseas connections of many Israelis have made it relatively easy for them to emigrate. In 1981 the Israeli Ministry of Labour and Social Welfare reported that over the previous ten years no fewer than 511,000 Israelis had left the country – a number that was much larger than the number of immigrants in the same period.[29] Emigration continued over the next two decades. Several hundred thousand Israelis now live in the United States and tens of thousands more live in other countries such as Germany, the Netherlands and South Africa. Most were economic migrants. Since 2000 the recession in the Israeli economy and the growth of unemployment, particularly in the high-tech sector, has led many to seek work elsewhere. A reasonable expectation is that such emigration is likely to increase should the current recession deepen – as seems probable in the event of a continuation of the recent level of political violence.

Against this background some Israeli demographers have sounded alarm bells. The foremost exponent of the so-called 'demographic doomsday' is Professor Arnon Soffer of the University of Haifa. In July 2001 he told the Knesset Foreign Affairs and Defence Committee that by 2020 Jews were

27

likely to account for only 42 per cent of the total population in Israel, the West Bank and Gaza. Even within Israel proper, i.e. within the 1967 borders, he projected that the non-Jewish population would amount to nearly a third of the total. Soffer said that the current demographic situation represented a 'threat to Israel's existence'.

Such projections have fed the political programmes of both left and right in Israel. Soffer himself called for unilateral Israeli withdrawal behind a security border of walls and fences – what has come to be known in Israel as 'separation'. Ran Cohen, a Knesset member representing the leftist Meretz Party, commented that Soffer's figures had 'an element of hysteria' but he nevertheless argued that they demonstrated that 'the vision of the Greater Land of Israel is a danger to Israel as a Jewish and democratic state'.[30] An Arab Knesset member denounced the discussion as 'racist' and the Egyptian newspaper *al-Ahram* suggested that such talk might be a prelude to the so-called 'transfer' of Arabs to beyond the Jordan.[31]

This idea was indeed raised by former Brigadier-General Effi Eitam in a discussion at a strategic think-tank in Herzliya in December 2001, in which Soffer participated. Eitam, a member of the National Religious Party, who became its leader and Minister of National Infrastructures in Ariel Sharon's Cabinet in 2002, has been a vocal advocate of the notion of 'transfer' – which, according to a public opinion poll published in March 2002, was favoured by no fewer than 46 per cent of the Jewish population of Israel.[32] No doubt this extraordinary percentage in favour of a policy that is, under international law, a war crime, was a reflection of the specific mood of extreme anger and frustration in the face of the crescendo of suicide bombings at the time the poll was taken. But it also reflects the underlying demographic anxieties of ordinary Israelis as well as of policymakers. Hence, no doubt, the decision of the Prime Minister's Office to summon Soffer to address the directors-general of government ministries.

Soffer is by no means alone in his predictions. Sergio DellaPergola of the Hebrew University of Jerusalem, perhaps the leading Israeli demographer, reckons that on medium projections of likely rates of natural increase and migration, Israel, even if it withdrew from all the occupied territories, would still have such a large non-Jewish population within fifty years that the likely result would be severe internal political conflict and possible partition of what remained of Israel.[33]

Of course, as these and other professional demographers warn us: all population projections, particularly long-range ones, are hazardous and, viewed historically, most turn out to be erroneous. But that should not lead to a total suspension of judgement. In this case, many of the core assumptions on which the projections are based seem quite stable: mass Jewish immigration to Israel is almost certainly a phenomenon of the past, given that the overwhelming majority of Diaspora Jews now live in stable liberal democracies with significantly higher per capita national incomes than Israel. Moreover, even if the Palestinian Arabs were over the next generation to undergo a demographic transition, and even if, *mirabile dictu*, the decline in the Israeli Jewish rate of natural increase were to be arrested, Palestinians would still greatly outnumber Jews in Palestine/Israel, considered as a whole, for the foreseeable future.

Zionism, in other words, is in the process of losing the demographic race. The implications of this defeat, when considered in broader socio-economic, geographical-ecological and cultural-political contexts, will be explored in what follows.

2 Society

From its early years Zionism was driven by a social no less than a demographic imperative. In particular the *halutzim* (pioneers), who arrived in Palestine in substantial numbers after 1904, adhered to the socialist-Zionist ideology formulated by Marxist thinkers such as Ber Borokhov. He called for an inversion of the Jewish social pyramid characteristic of the Diaspora. The socialist Zionists considered the occupational distribution of the Jewish people, consisting in the main of petty bourgeois traders and craftsmen and an almost non-existent peasantry, to be deeply unhealthy. Instead, they called for the creation of a new Jewish working class in Palestine, of which the base should be an agricultural society organized on collective principles. The Jews were to be 'productivized': they would be transformed from parasitic quasi-capitalists into solid labourers and producers. The ideals of dignity of labour and of return to the land chimed with the thinking of the previous wave of settlers from Russia, many of whom had been influenced by Russian populism of the 1860s and 70s. Both socialist and non-socialist Zionists idealized rural society and invented a mythic-heroic type of the new Hebrew farmer. Explaining why this society must be created in Palestine rather than anywhere else, Borokhov resorted to a contorted rationalization, based on the notion that there was a 'stychic' or natural economic basis for Jewish settlement there that existed nowhere else. He argued that

> The natives of *Eretz Yisrael* [the Land of Israel] have no independent economic or cultural character … are not a single nation, nor will they constitute a single nation for a long time … It is the Jewish immigrants who will undertake the forces of production of *Eretz Yisrael* and the local population will assimilate economically and culturally to the Jews.[1]

Less formalistic Marxists among the Zionists came to believe in a natural harmony, an almost mystic communion, between the *halutzim* and the soil of the land of Israel.

The individual and collective models for socialist Zionism were respectively the sabra (native-born) Jewish agricultural worker and the kibbutz. The sabra, according to the Israeli social historian Oz Almog, was 'not [a] biological … but [a] cultural' phenomenon, a member of a generational unit, roughly stretching from the 1920s to the 1950s, 'identified not by country of birth, but rather by affiliation to an institution that imprinted a specific culture'.[2] Superficially, the sabra was a democratic concept: any Jew born in the Land of Israel could qualify – and by this means shed the unwanted skin of a Diaspora past. But all this was ideological pap for the masses. The reality was that the sabra generation was a restricted elite that had more in common with the Soviet nomenklatura than with a genuinely open society.

The central figure of Zionist myth, like the Soviet 'New Man' and the Aryan 'Blond Beast', the sabra was a propaganda idol invested with the ideology's values, hopes and dreams. According to the novelist Haim Guri, the sabras 'startled the midwives who saw them being born with a monkey wrench and pistol in hand'.[3] Another writer suggested that the model figures were Yitzhak Sadeh (founder of the Palmach, the pre-state underground commando force) and Gary Cooper.[4] The sabra was the strong, silent type, physically and mentally the antithesis of the supposedly weedy, garrulous, cosmopolitan, over-intellectual Diaspora Jew.

In truth, this new Jew was not very Jewish. Almog dubs him a 'gentile Jew' – though by this he means something very different from Isaac Deutscher's 'non-Jewish Jew'.[5] Like the anti-Zionist Deutscher, the sabra was determinedly, defiantly secular. But there the resemblance stopped, for the sabra was taught to despise everything about the Diaspora Jew who was frequently presented to him in the shape of anti-Semitic stereotypes. The Diasporic condition was depicted as a kind of disease, exile as a form of leprosy. Hence the contempt with which sabras viewed survivors of the Nazi genocide. Adopting a phrase first used by the writer David Frishman in the 1930s, David Ben-Gurion, Israel's first Prime Minister, called them 'human dust'.[6]

Yet out of such unpromising clay the new, regenerated Zionist form could yet be fashioned. Although most sabras were native-born, some youngsters born overseas were so thoroughly socialized as to become worthy of membership in the elite – though it was a tougher challenge for the non-native-born. Moshe Sharett, Levi Eshkol and Shimon Peres probably all made the grade; Abba Eban and Menahem Begin never did. How could one tell? It was a matter of style, of dress, of speech and an indefinable sense of belonging to the same cohort. As in all clubs, certain groups were generally excluded: sabras were almost invariably Ashkenazim, not Sephardim. And the godless spirit of the sabra shut out most religious Jews, even the Zionist minority among them, from full membership.

In the popular imagination the sabra was, almost by definition, male. In real life, according to Almog, he was sexually puritanical and, in spite of his anti-establishment outlook, more conventional in his attitude to the family than the parental generation. An upbringing in the children's house of the kibbutz induced a kind of incest taboo in relation to the entire cohort.

Sabra society was spartan in almost every sense. Dancing, popular in the cities, was frowned on by Zionist 'gatekeepers' – except in the ideologically acceptable form of the collective folk dance such as the *hora* (a fusion of Romanian peasant and Hasidic dance forms). The elite military units, particularly the Palmach, were largely sabra in composition, wholly so in ethos. Almog calls them 'socialization workshops that heightened the typical sabra trademarks of language and dress'.[7] After the establishment of the state, the sabra 'military aristocracy' developed into a political ruling caste that gradually displaced the pre-state generation of whom the last representatives in power were Menahem Begin and Yitzhak Shamir.

The schooling of the sabra was a concentrated process of brainwashing. In Zionist history schoolbooks from the 1930s onwards, not only were all doctrines hostile or contradictory to Zionism expunged, but, according to Almog, 'even beliefs and ideologies that were simply different from Zionist ones were left out'. The overriding goal of Zionist education, as of the immensely influential youth movements, was to integrate the pupil into the *Yishuv* (the Jewish community in pre-1948 Palestine) 'in a way that will never allow him to detach himself from the fabric of the common destiny' – as one textbook writer put it. 'Hebrew culture,' writes Almog, 'was glorified and made central to world culture; it was the standard against which all other cultures were compared.' Homogeneity and obliteration of the self were allied to such ethnocentrism. The sabra was moulded into a conformist who, according to Almog, 'had limited capacity to observe his culture "from the outside" and a limited critical faculty'.[8] Jettisoning the traditional Jewish cultural legacy, the sabra was an anti-intellectual. He did not attend university and did not greatly value the life of the mind. Occasionally he might write or read lyrical poetry, but the passionate ideological debates of the immigrant generation of socialist Zionists were alien to him.

Even such a brief outline of the *Weltanschauung* of the sabra evokes a bygone age. The sabra generation has died out, as have the social and cultural values with which it was associated. Even many of those who lament the trend admit its reality. The prominent Israeli literary critic Gershon Shaked, for example, wrote in 1998:

> What happened to the revolution of Zionist
> culture? Where has it gone and disappeared to?
> Why are its creators ashamed of their work ...?
> ... Why has their resolve weakened and why are
> they undergoing a religious revival and returning
> to ghetto culture or 'descending' from Israel to
> emigrate to the West and its culture?

Shaked mourns the demise of a distinctive Israeli secular culture. The loss of collective Zionist values, he believes, has produced a generation of rootless individualists. 'The individual Israeli is no longer capable of finding his "Israeliness", for it disappeared while he was trying to flee from it. What remains is a people with a blurred image, living a secular life, smitten by guilt feelings for a lost "Yiddishkeit" which it does not know how to define for itself.'[9]

The cultural world of the sabra has vanished because the social conditions that gave rise to it have gone. Indeed, they were never securely established. The socialist Zionists came to Palestine to create a rural utopia. But Palestinian Jewish society remained highly urbanized (see Figure 5). It has been estimated that in 1880 under 1 per cent of the Jewish population was rural. Of the 25,000 immigrants of the first *aliya* following 1881 who remained in the country in 1900, some 80 per cent were settled in towns rather than on the land.[10]

Figure 5 **Urban/rural proportions of Jews in Mandatory Palestine/Israel, 1880–2002**

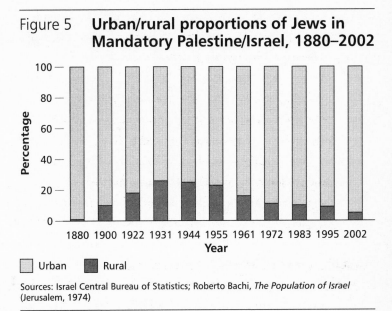

Sources: Israel Central Bureau of Statistics; Roberto Bachi, *The Population of Israel* (Jerusalem, 1974)

Altogether in 1900 no more than about 10 per cent of the Jewish population of Palestine was rural. After 1908 the Zionists made a concentrated effort, aided by large-scale capital investment, to settle Jews on the land. In proportional demographic terms, at least, the results were not all that impressive. By 1922 18 per cent of the Jewish population was rural and by 1944 25 per cent. After the advent of the State of Israel, the rural proportion of the Jewish population plummeted; in 2002, by the same measure as in the pre-1948 period, it was probably no more than 5 per cent.[11]

The collapse of the Zionist agrarian vision becomes even clearer if we measure not by residence but by share of national product. In 1922 agriculture constituted 14 per cent of total output in the Jewish sector of the Palestinian economy. By 1947 the agricultural share had declined to 12 per cent. In 2002, although agricultural output had increased greatly, the sector's share of total Israeli GDP was no more than 2 per cent. Citrus production, in particular, which alone generated 74 per cent of Palestine's export earnings in 1939 and 63 per cent of Israel's in 1949, has dropped precipitously as a proportion of foreign trade in general and of agricultural production. The land area covered by citrus orchards has fallen by more than half and is now at the same level as in the 1950s. Meanwhile the number of agricultural workers has diminished steadily – from 91,700 in 1969 to 47,900 in 2000.[12]

Politically, socialist Zionists dominated the *Yishuv* from the early 1930s to the first election victory of Menahem Begin in 1977. Socially, they sought to perpetuate their value system through youth movements, a national-labour Hebrew education stream, through the so-called 'party key' spoils system of 'jobs for the boys', through the allocation of immigration certificates (devolved by the mandatory government to the Jewish Agency), as well as by means of other centrally controlled favours.

Economically, the dominance of the socialist Zionists was expressed in such institutions as the Histadrut labour confederation, the kibbutzim and moshavim, and cooperative marketing systems. They sought to define a distinct Jewish economy by concentrating a great part of agricultural land ownership in the hands of the Jewish National Fund, by socialized control of key enterprises, and by the so-called

'struggle for Hebrew labour'. This was waged both exter-
nally against low-wage Arab labour and internally against
Jewish private employers. It was never completely successful
since some Jewish employers would not comply, many non-
Jewish ones, such as the Haifa oil refinery, employed both
Jews and Arabs, and the mandatory government tried to
maintain some rough ethnic proportionality in its employment policies.

In purely economic terms, the socialist sector's role in the
growth of the mandatory Jewish economy has commonly
been exaggerated. It was less the socialist Zionists who
brought about the initial take-off by the industrial economy
of Jewish Palestine than the private-enterprise entrepreneurs
who arrived from central Europe in the mid-1920s and from
Germany in the mid-1930s, the latter wave in particular
bringing with them business skills, capital, technical inven-
tiveness, and modern industrial management experience.
Between 1932 and 1940 total production in the Jewish sector nearly tripled (see Figure 6).[13] During the war there was
a further spurt as a result of the big increase in demand generated by British war needs. In his painstaking examination
of the 'divided economy' of mandatory Palestine, Jacob Metzer concludes that the share of the non-private, labour-con-
trolled sector of the Jewish economy under the mandate
probably did not exceed 20 per cent – and Haim Barkai has
determined that this remained true even in the early, supposedly ultra-socialist years of the Israeli economy.[14]

The egalitarian ethos of socialist Zionism, which, of
course, in practice, excluded Palestinian and later Israeli

39

Figure 6   **Net domestic product of Jewish and Arab economies in Palestine, 1923–1947**

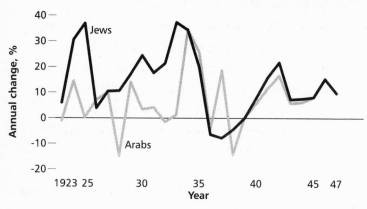

Source: Jacob Metzer, *The Divided Economy of Mandatory Palestine* (Cambridge, 1998).

Arabs, faded under the impact of mass immigration of Jews from Africa and Asia. From the 1950s onwards a quasi-ethnic division emerged in Israeli society, whereby Jews of non-European origin, often strangely called *edot ha-mizrah* (oriental communities) though their largest single component consisted of Jews from the Maghreb, were submerged as an under-class. This type of class division has probably lessened somewhat with time. In an analysis of class mobility in the period 1974 to 1991, Meir Yaish argues that 'the ethnic/national cleavage in Israel appears to have played a less important role over time in the allocation of Israeli men to class positions'.[15] Other research has shown some decline in ethnic endogamy: in other words, comparing the 1950s and 1990s, more Ashkenazim and Sephardim are marrying outside their groups. On the other hand, a study by Barbara Okun concludes:

> Despite these declines, ethnic endogamy remains a significant and central feature of marriage behaviour ... Implications of declines in, but continuing salience of, ethnic endogamy are significant, as interethnic conflict and related socio-economic inequality are among the prime domestic concerns in Israel today.[16]

Gershon Shafir and Yoav Peled, in their book *Being Israeli*, point to a number of studies suggesting that ethnicity and class still march together.[17] The continuing political salience of ethnicity was clearly signalled in the parliamentary elections of 1999 by the unprecedented success of parties based on the support of Jews from Russia and from Arab lands.

Although so-called ethnicity among Jews seems to play less of a role in class positioning in Israel, the general perception is that economic inequality in the country has increased greatly in recent years. The Israeli National Insurance Institute ranked Israel second only to the United States in the developed world for inequality in net income (household income after transfers and taxes) in 2000.[18] A parliamentary committee report presented to the Israeli government in December 2002 similarly concluded that Israel was surpassed only by the USA in terms of social gaps in income, ownership of property, distribution of capital, access to education, consumption patterns – and in the prevalence of poverty.[19]

Ira Sharkansky of the Hebrew University of Jerusalem, however, has argued that the common stress on Israel's growing 'social gap' is misplaced and that 'Israel's level of income equality more or less reflects its level of economic development.'[20] Sharkansky's conclusions are offered some support by a model developed by Robert Lerman of the Urban Institute in Washington.[21] Disputing the common perception of increasing inequality in the United States, he proposes, as a heuristic path, the case of equality trends in Germany between 1988 and 1998. During that period, of course, West Germany absorbed East Germany. Most people would agree that any analysis using West Germany in 1988 as a base of comparison with the whole of Germany in 1998 would be misleading. Yet, Lerman argues, much discussion of inequality trends in the United States makes a similar mistake by failing to take account of large-scale immigration. The same argument might well be applied with even greater force to Israel, which has absorbed nearly three million immigrants since 1948 and over a million since 1988. To apply Lerman's argument, the 20 per cent increase in population as a result of the recent wave of immigration from the CIS was equivalent to the Federal Republic's absorption of East Germany. Yet Israel today is often compared for socio-economic purposes with a base of Israel ten or twenty years ago. According to this approach, comparisons of inequality over time may be grossly misleading in countries of mass immigration, most notably Israel. The remarkable success of many Russian immigrants of recent years in integrating economically into Israeli society may suggest that Lerman's view is a realistic one. Nevertheless, it is beyond argument that Israel today, and particularly its affluent heartland around Tel Aviv, is a consumer society that the spartan zealots of the second *aliya* (1904–14) would have shunned.

The fading away of the Zionist agrarian socialist dream is epitomized by the decline in recent decades of the kibbutz – the *polis* of the *Yishuv*, as it has been called.[22] From modest origins in the years 1909–14, the kibbutzim grew mightily in numbers and prestige in the course of the mandatory period and came to be regarded as the home of the Zionist elite. By 1948 they had 54,208 inhabitants in 159 settlements. Although they maintained their social standing and political influence in the early years of the state, they played only a marginal role in the absorption of new immigrants. In particular, they failed to attract or integrate significant numbers of non-European Jews. Most Jewish refugees from North Africa and the Middle East settled in towns or in moshavim (cooperative smallholder settlements). The kibbutz, as a result, remained an overwhelmingly Ashkenazi movement. In absolute terms, the number of kibbutzniks increased until the mid-1980s when it reached 127,000. But since 1985, when the kibbutz movement suffered a massive debt crisis, the population has declined in every year but one. At the end of 1999 there were 103,000 permanent residents in 275 kibbutzim. As a proportion of the total Jewish population, kibbutzniks dwindled from around 8 per cent in 1948 to barely 2 per cent today. The decline was not confined to the collectivist kibbutzim: the moshavim too suffered a decline in population and, in some cases, transformation into privatized communities.

Some kibbutzim have gone bankrupt. Others, such as Ramat Rahel near Jerusalem, were allowed to lease chunks of their land for housing developments, commercial centres or industrial parks – a process facilitated after 1992 by changes in the legal framework of land ownership that for the first time created something like a free market in real estate in Israel. A few kibbutzim, such as Kfar Ruppin, turned into holding companies in which members were shareholders. Others rented out empty apartments on the open market.

Meanwhile many of the characteristic social norms of earlier years disappeared or atrophied: absence of money wages, non-specialization of labour, non-employment of outside labour, collective dining halls, entertainments, and children's residences. In their place came privatization, differential salaries, incentive systems, productivity bonuses, overtime payments, ownership of private cars and other consumer durables, credit cards, personal pension schemes, and reliance on outside (often Arab) labour. By 1999 62 per cent of all workers in kibbutzim were hired hands.[23] The last kibbutz to retain communal sleeping arrangements for children decided to do away with the practice in 1996. Weekly general assemblies, once arenas of impassioned ideological debate, have dwindled into formalism or disappeared altogether, to be replaced by elected councils. Kibbutz production today is more industrial than agricultural. An estimated 40 per cent of kibbutz-born youngsters currently choose to move away. As the rising generation leave for army service, higher education, and jobs in the city, some kibbutzim have degenerated almost into geriatric ghettos, to the outward eye little distinguishable from Century Village and other retirement complexes in Florida.

Kibbutzim still wield disproportionate political influence: they constitute about 17 per cent of members of the Labour Party.[24] But their historic role as a political vanguard has vanished. A survey in 1998 found that only a minority of kibbutz members believed that the institution had a future.[25] Small wonder that one recent commentator concluded: 'The condition of the kibbutz is terminal.'[26] 'The vision of a new human being,' a more sympathetic observer writes, 'a just society, a better world, as proclaimed by the prophets of Israel, has gone the way of previous utopian visions. Human nature has triumphed over idealism; ambition has proved stronger than altruism; individuality has vanquished communal responsibility.'[27]

Instead of a federation of Hebrew peasant communes, the Zionists created an industrialized, urbanized society. What remains of the original Zionist ambition? One thing: the Jewishness of the state. But that too is now under threat, both demographically and in other ways.

Of course, the Jewish society in Palestine did not emerge in a vacuum but side-by-side and in some crucial ways in an inextricable relationship with a Palestinian Arab economy and society that exhibited very different characteristics. In the late Ottoman and mandatory periods this was overwhelmingly a rural society. In 1880 an estimated 79 per cent of the Arab population was rural and the percentage is even higher if we consider Muslim Arabs alone. In 1931 70 per cent of the Arab population was still rural and 57 per cent of the labour force was engaged in agriculture. Throughout this period there was a continuing process of urbanization but even in 1946 64 per cent of Palestinian Arabs were rural, most of them peasants. The Palestinian Arab economy contained a small industrial sector that showed some vitality in the mandatory period but overall agriculture remained dominant: as late as 1946 its contribution to total production in the Arab sector was nearly four times larger than that of manufacturing industry.

Palestinian Arab peasant agriculture during this period came under intense pressure as a result of rapid population growth. It was also affected by the growth of a capital-intensive, cash-crop, citrus industry. Indebtedness, particularly of sharecroppers, grew to such an extent that by 1931 the liabilities of the average Palestinian peasant equalled his annual income. A series of natural calamities in the 1920s and 1930s added to agrarian distress: locust, fieldmouse, and starling plagues and several years of drought.[28] These developments drew the rural Arab population away from near-subsistence agriculture in the hill regions, down into the coastal plain where they worked as labourers in the towns or as employees on citrus plantations, or sometimes a combination of the two. Arab urbanization was certainly accelerated by the effects of Jewish land purchase and by the spin-off effects of Jewish economic growth. But these were probably not the main causes of the rural–urban migration of Palestinians in this period. Such movement was a general phenomenon throughout the Middle East and beyond, one that was intensified in Palestine by the phenomenally high rate of population growth, particularly among the Muslim peasantry.

Although the amount of land transferred to Jewish owner-ship between 1881 and 1948 was small relative to the total area of Palestine, not much more than 6 per cent of the country, this included a large part of the richest agricultural land in Palestine (see Maps 1 and 2). Land purchase was, of course, one of the nodal points connecting the two, other-wise largely separate, Jewish and Arab economies and as a re-sult gives us a special window into shared and competing values. The dominant figure in this story was neither the Zionist nor the Arab nationalist: he was *homo economicus*.

In his examination of the land problem in Palestine be-tween 1917 and 1939, Kenneth Stein showed that neither Arab nationalist exhortation nor British official intervention could halt the process of land alienation by Arab landowners, some non-Palestinian, but most Palestinian. The only limita-tion on the ability of the Zionists to buy land, he concludes, was the amount of capital they could make available for the purpose. Arab opposition to land sales was frequently voiced by the very people who were themselves selling land to the Zionists. There was a certain economic logic in this since political hostility to land sales tended to drive up prices. To that extent Arab nationalism may have somewhat constrained Jewish land purchase. But the Zionists never found a lack of ready sellers. Indeed, as Stein showed, the sellers of land in-cluded a remarkably large proportion of members of the leadership of the Palestinian Arab nationalist movement.[29]

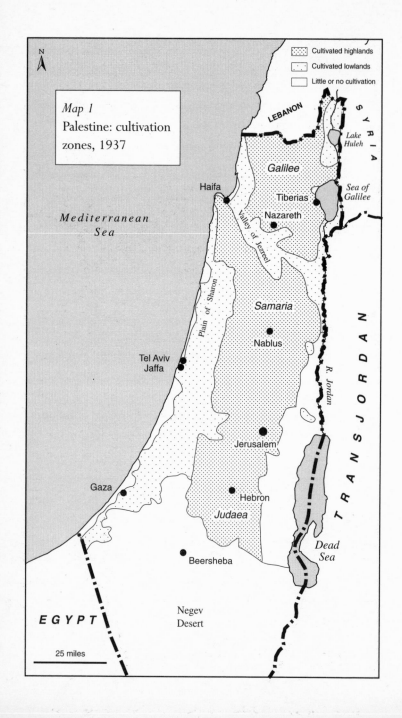

Map 1
Palestine: cultivation
zones, 1937

Cultivated highlands
Cultivated lowlands
Little or no cultivation

N

LEBANON

SYRIA

Lake
Huleh

Galilee

Haifa

Tiberias

Sea of
Galilee

Nazareth

Mediterranean
Sea

Valley of Jezreel

Plain of Sharon

Samaria

Nablus

T R A N S J O R D A N

Tel Aviv
Jaffa

R. Jordan

Jerusalem

Gaza

Hebron

Judaea

Dead
Sea

Beersheba

EGYPT

Negev
Desert

25 miles

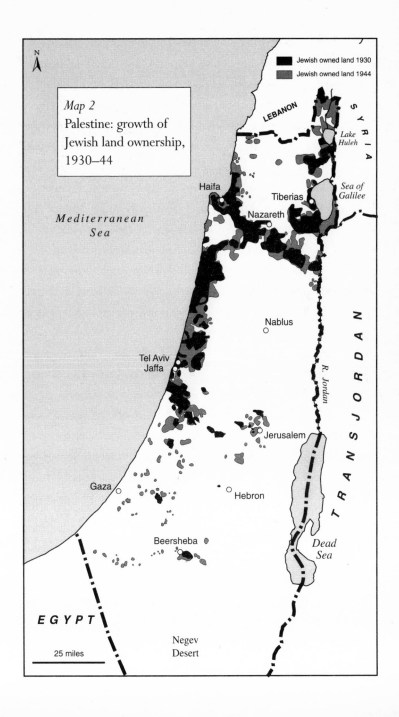

Map 2
Palestine: growth of
Jewish land ownership,
1930–44

Jewish owned land 1930
Jewish owned land 1944

N

LEBANON

SYRIA

Lake
Huleh

Sea of
Galilee

Haifa

Tiberias

*Mediterranean
Sea*

Nazareth

Nablus

Tel Aviv
Jaffa

R. Jordan

Jerusalem

TRANSJORDAN

Gaza

Hebron

*Dead
Sea*

Beersheba

EGYPT

Negev
Desert

25 miles

As for the British, they, like their Ottoman predecessors, but with no greater success, attempted to limit Jewish land purchase by a succession of legal enactments, the so-called 'protection of cultivators ordinances'. These had little effect and even, according to Stein, stimulated further sales by raising peasants' expectations that land once sold to Jews would be returned to the original owners by the government. The ordinances were issued one after another – but were bowled over like skittles by the collusive efforts of willing sellers and eager buyers. British officials became increasingly exasperated by their failure to protect Arab peasants from finding the land they worked sold beneath their feet – or indeed their failure to prevent peasant-landowners themselves being obliged by indebtedness to sell their land to Jews, often through third parties.

The underlying social forces and attitudes involved emerge clearly from the controversy in the early 1930s over the so-called 'landless Arab inquiry'. This was one of a series of investigations launched by the government following anti-Jewish riots in 1929. The Shaw Commission, appointed to look into their causes, recommended in December 1929 that a special inquiry be conducted into the land problem in Palestine. This was carried out by Sir John Hope-Simpson, who reported in 1930 that there was very little room left in Palestine for expansion of Jewish colonization. Indeed, he said, 'if all the cultivable land in Palestine were divided up among the Arab agricultural population, there would not be enough to provide every family with a decent livelihood'. And he added, 'there is not room for a single additional settler if the standard of life of the *fellaheen* is to remain at its present level'. He conceded that, if the government pursued an active policy of agricultural development, that might create room for an additional 20,000 families of settlers, but, pending such a policy, he recommended that all further Jewish agricultural settlement be prohibited.[30]

Hope-Simpson's report provoked outrage from the Zionists, who complained that it was biased and founded on faulty statistical assumptions, in particular unreasonable estimates of the amount of cultivable land and of the minimum *lot viable* for a peasant family. Whereas Hope-Simpson estimated the total cultivable area of Palestine at 6.5 million metric dunams,[31] the Jewish Agency argued that the true cultivable area was nearly double that. The Zionists maintained that the government's definition of 'cultivable land' as that which could be worked by an 'average Palestinian cultivator['s] labour and resources' was too restrictive. Instead, they urged, the definition should be based on the level of productivity to which the *fellah* could be brought 'by credits and guidance ... [from] the government and by the example of Jewish colonization'.[32]

Even at this stage, Jewish agricultural productivity was, as a result of much greater capital investment, far higher than Arab. A government report in 1930 showed an average yield on Arab lands of 70 kilos per dunam of wheat and 59 per dunam of barley. The comparable figures for Jewish-worked lands were 111 of wheat and 153 to 177 of barley. Overall, the Jewish farmer was reckoned to produce on average twice as much as the Arab – though with greater costs of production.[33]

The question of rural landlessness could be settled only by a further detailed inquiry for which it was proposed to gather data in the 1931 census – but, as we have seen, this was dropped by the government on the insistence of the Zionists. A separate inquiry was therefore launched by the government's newly appointed Director of Development, Lewis French, who was instructed to draw up a register of landless Arabs. Some 4,500 claims for inclusion were lodged within a few months. But the results were embarrassing for the government. By April 1932 only seventy-two claims had been finally judged legitimate. As French wearily reported, 'With the best will in the world, the investigation of claims *prima facie* sustainable must be a slow and tedious process.'[34] His forecast proved correct: in spite of great efforts, a total of only 664 claims had been approved by 1936. The government took responsibility for resettling these claimants but by 1939, when the project was closed down, a total of only seventy-four families had been resettled out of 899 ultimately classified as landless.[35]

One reason for these nugatory results was the refusal of the Palestine Arab Executive, the chief nationalist body, to have anything to do with the scheme, which it viewed as a tacit endorsement of the mandatory power's pro-Zionist policy. Another cause of the project's failure was the paying-off by the Zionists of many potential applicants. But the chief explanation was the narrow official conception of landlessness. The government defined 'landless Arabs' as persons 'who can be shown to have been displaced from the lands which they occupied in consequence of the lands falling into

Jewish hands, and who have not obtained other holdings on which they can establish themselves or other equally satisfactory occupation'.[36] Since most of the peasants who were displaced did not starve to death but found some other form of livelihood, often in towns, they did not qualify for registration as 'landless'. French himself tacitly admitted the futility of his computational effort when he none the less maintained that Jewish settlement was leading to large-scale displacement of Arab peasants. Notwithstanding the difficulty of finding landless Arabs, he argued, the very fact that there were any at all proved that no surplus cultivable land remained in Palestine, since 'if there were available areas of such land ... the Arabs who were displaced from the land by the Jews would already have transferred themselves there'.[37] He concluded apocalyptically that 'if the process of dispossession continues, in another three or four decades the Arab peasant proprietor will become almost extinct'.[38] French urged that existing legislation to protect cultivators be strengthened. Further such measures were enacted – but to little avail. Even after 1940, when the government introduced draconian land-transfer regulations that supposedly limited the unrestricted transfer of land to Jews to a mere 5 per cent of the area of the country, Jewish land acquisition continued on a substantial scale.

Metzer argues that the actual number of peasants displaced was certainly larger than the number entered in the register and he makes a bold attempt to estimate the true number on the basis of admittedly inadequate data. He computes that

displacement of tenants caused by
intercommunal land transactions could at most
have accounted for half the relative decline of
employment in Arab agriculture between 1921
and 1945, the rest being employment shifts of
former peasant owner-cultivators who had sold
their [own] land to Jews, and of others: peasants,
tenants, and wage earners who moved from
domestic agriculture to different industries
(including employment by Jewish farmers).[39]

Metzer links this exit from the land persuasively to the larger
structural changes that were producing rural–urban migration, particularly towards the coastal region.

The search for the landless Arab, as things turned out, was
as futile as the quest for the Wandering Jew. In the light of
subsequent experience in Palestine, we may conclude that
the reports of both Hope-Simpson and French were vitiated,
like British official attitudes in general, by an incorrigibly
static view of Palestinian agricultural society. Another government report in 1930 had conceded that 'the foremost
need of the [Arab] agricultural industry is rationalisation'.
But it continued: 'The rural population, which forms the
bulk of the indigenous population, could not easily be indus-
trialised even if there were industries to absorb it. It is therefore essential to secure to this rural population in its present
occupation at least the minimum of subsistence.'[40] The committee 'strongly deprecate[d] any attempts to produce the
desired result [greater productivity] which might end in

tempting the farmer away from the soil and turning him into a black-coated effendi'.[41]

With hindsight it is plain to see that there was no such thing as a static *lot viable*. The vast increase in agricultural land use and productivity in the country over succeeding decades proves that. More sophisticated British observers understood the point. Eric Mills, for example, wrote in 1931: 'The application of growing human intelligence and experience obviously changes the *lot viable*. It seems to be necessary to concentrate skilled attention on the agricultural possibilities in the hill country if the *lot viable* is, on average, to be reduced with an improving standard of life.'[42] Although Arab agricultural productivity lagged steadily further behind Jewish, it too improved: between 1922 and 1945 Arab agricultural production grew by an average 6 per cent per annum and agricultural product per worker by an average annual rate of 4.1 per cent.

Modern capital-intensive methods were particularly applied in citrus plantations by both Jews and Arabs. Thus by the late 1930s citrus fruit plantations, which covered only 2 per cent of the area cultivated by Arabs, were employing 20 per cent of Arab agricultural workers and generating 28 per cent of total Arab agricultural output.[43] Until 1936 many Arabs worked in Jewish-owned citrus plantations. Thereafter, as a result of the Arab revolt and Jewish labour union pressure, this key sector of the Jewish economy turned increasingly to the use of Jewish labour.

In some measure Jewish land purchase undoubtedly contributed to what has been termed the 'proletarianization' of

Arab peasants. But this was merely part of the general dislocation of Palestinian society arising from migration from the hills to the plains, from urbanization, and from the rapid increase in literacy under British rule. The process of social fragmentation quickened as a result of the decapitation of a significant part of the traditional political elite of landowning and office-holding notables in the course of British repression of the Arab revolt between 1936 and 1939. The roots of the woefully disoriented, disorganized, and ineffective response of Palestinian Arab society to the challenge presented to them in 1947/8 stretched far back into the social history of the British mandate.

Defeat and exile in 1948 brought about the virtual disintegration of Palestinian society. The old divisions between nomads and settled population, between notables and peasantry, between town and country, between Muslims and Christians, became less significant. They were overlaid by the division between refugees and non-refugees, and that between Israeli Arabs and those in the surrounding Arab states.

The period 1949 to 1967 marked the high-water mark of the Zionist attempt to create a hermetic Jewish economy and society in Palestine. As a result of the continuing state of war and of the Arab economic boycott, Israel's land borders were virtually sealed against movement of people or goods. Mass immigration fed Israel's labour needs and helped her achieve a rapid rate of economic growth. Yet even before 1967 there were some signs that social pressures were militating against the maintenance of a relatively homogeneous Jewish society. In the early 1960s Israeli Arabs, hitherto mainly peasants, began to join the broader Israeli labour market. Many learned Hebrew and a few entered the urban professions.

The Israeli occupation of the West Bank and Gaza in 1967 added a new line of internal division to Palestinian society, that between residents of the Israeli-occupied territories and the rest. Yet in some ways the 1967 war marked a crucial stage in the reconstitution of a Palestinian Arab community. The end of the rigid separation that had characterized the years 1949 to 1967, and continuing discrimination against Arabs in Israel, brought a gradual rapprochement between Palestinians in the West Bank and Gaza and Israeli Arabs. The 'open bridges' policy across the Jordan, espoused by the then Israeli Defence Minister, Moshe Dayan, maintained economic, social and cultural connections between Palestinians in the occupied territories and those in surrounding countries, particularly Jordan. The creation of the Palestinian Authority in 1994 accelerated the process, although it is by no means complete.

One indicator of its incompleteness is the small number of 'mixed' marriages between refugee and non-refugee Palestinians. For example, according to official records, in Gaza in 1995 45 per cent of marriages were between refugees, 46 per cent between non-refugees, and only 9 per cent between a refugee and a non-refugee. This in an area where the population is divided about 70/30 refugee/non-refugee.[44]

Palestinian society, in so far as it has been reconstituted in the West Bank and Gaza, is characterized by a high degree of economic dependency – in several senses. Because of the low average age, high unemployment rate, and low female participation in the labour force, each worker has a large number of dependants.[45] In the second quarter of 2002 the average number of people dependent on each wage-earner in the West Bank and Gaza was 7.6 (in Gaza alone the figure was 9.4).[46] Secondly, more than 40 per cent of the population, still classified as refugees, rely on the support of UNRWA (the United Nations Relief and Works Agency for Palestinian Refugees in the Near East, established in December 1949) and other international and private welfare agencies. Thirdly, the Palestinian Authority itself could not continue to function without the help it receives from international donors. According to a recent World Bank report 'at $195 per person per annum, aid flows to the West Bank and Gaza represent one of the highest per capita official development assistance [programmes] anywhere in the world'.[47] But the most important dependency is that on Israel, a connection that, quite apart from the obviously unequal military/ political relationship, also takes an economic form that is sometimes not sufficiently appreciated.

Here we have two societies living side by side and to some extent economically intertwined. First, Israel, no longer a Hebrew-speaking Arcadia but a relatively advanced industrial society, in some ways a post-industrial, techno-service economy, with a GNP of about $120 billion and an average per capita income of $19,000, i.e. approaching European Union levels. Secondly, Palestine, that is to say the areas of the West Bank and Gaza administered by the Palestinian Authority.

This has a GNP of under $5 billion (in 2000) and a per capita income less than one-tenth that of Israel. Although 46 per cent of the population is still classified as rural, only about 13 per cent depend on agriculture as their primary source of income (though that proportion may have increased as a result of recent events).[48] Agriculture today contributes only 8 per cent of Palestinian GDP (although the World Bank may underestimate the value of much subsistence agriculture).[49] One cause of the decline of agriculture has been Israeli restriction of Palestinian access to water in the West Bank (rejection of applications for permits to drill wells). But the main reason is the general trend towards urbanization. The trade deficit of about 50 per cent is almost exclusively with Israel and the Palestinian Authority depends critically on Israeli transfers of indirect taxes and customs duties collected on imported goods destined for the Palestinian areas (transfers that have been suspended for most of the period since December 2000).

Palestinian dependency on Israel is most evident in another sphere. Since 1967 these two economies have been bonded together in a wrestlers' embrace by one phenomenon in particular: Arab labour. Partly because of high population growth, partly because of the appetite of Israeli employers for, by Israeli standards, low-wage labour, and partly because of low public and private investment in the occupied territories (except in the new Israeli settlements and associated infrastructure projects), an ever-increasing proportion of the Palestinian labour force was drawn into work within the 'green line', the pre-1967 border of Israel.

By 1983 more than a third of the labour force of the West Bank and Gaza (74,000 out of 215,000) were working in Israel.[50] Those were the official figures issued by the Israeli Ministry of Labour but it was an open secret that there existed also an extensive underground labour economy. This drew in many thousands more Arab workers, often for wages and conditions that Israeli workers would not accept but that nevertheless proved irresistibly attractive to Palestinians whose earning potential at home was greatly inferior. According to the estimate of a World Bank economist, 'for workers with similar individual characteristics ... commuting to Israel added a 91 per cent premium to wages when compared to working in the West Bank and Gaza'.[51]

A poverty map of the West Bank and Gaza provides a neat illustration of the vital importance of work in Israel to the Palestinian economy: those areas with closest access to the central industrial dynamo of Israel and its jobs are the ones with the lowest rates of poverty; the more distant an area is from the Israeli labour market, the greater the level of poverty (see Map 3). Incidentally, this mirrors the incidence of poverty in Israel, which is similarly concentrated in so-called 'development towns' in the peripheral regions – such dead-end places as Yeruham in the Negev or Kiryat Shemona in the north-eastern *etzba* (finger).

Arab labour in Israel after 1967 was concentrated in certain sectors of the economy. The construction industry became almost wholly dependent on it. The Jewish settlements in the occupied territories, indeed, were largely built by Palestinian Arabs. The kibbutzim, as we have seen, hired

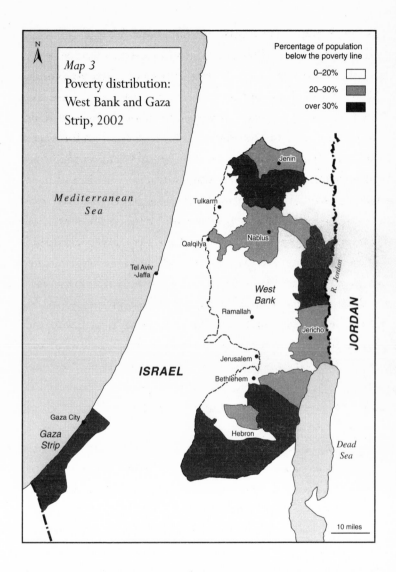

Map 3
Poverty distribution:
West Bank and Gaza
Strip, 2002

Percentage of population
below the poverty line

0–20%
20–30%
over 30%

Mediterranean
Sea

Jenin

Tulkarm

Qalqilya

Nablus

Tel Aviv
-Jaffa

West
Bank

Ramallah

R. Jordan

Jericho

JORDAN

ISRAEL

Jerusalem

Bethlehem

Gaza City

Gaza
Strip

Hebron

Dead
Sea

10 miles

increasing numbers of Arab labourers both in agriculture and in industrial plants. So did many of the Jewish settlements in the occupied territories that engaged in agriculture. The Israeli tourist industry too, a vital foreign-currency earner, employed large numbers of Palestinians. Even the clubs issued to Israeli soldiers during the first intifada were largely produced by Palestinian workers.[52] The security barrier constructed by Israel during the second intifada was erected in part by Arab and foreign labour.

The reaction of Israeli society to its growing dependence on Arab labour was ambivalent. There was considerable lamentation at the abandonment of the cherished ideal of Hebrew labour. Perhaps for this reason, between the early 1980s and 1994 the Israeli government attempted to reduce reliance on Palestinian workers. But high unemployment exacerbated political tension in the occupied territories, feeding the first intifada between 1987 and 1993. The buoyant Israeli economy of the 1990s exhibited an insatiable appetite for imported labour and after the first Oslo agreement the number of Palestinians working in Israel began to climb again.[53] After 1993, however, Palestinian workers were obliged to show identity documents and special permits at permanent checkpoints that were established, for the first time since the early days of the occupation, on or near the former 'green line'. There were frequent 'closures' after terrorist incidents but tens of thousands sneaked in by back roads and worked illegally for Israeli labour contractors who thereby avoided paying health insurance or social security taxes. The collusion on

Figure 7   **Palestinian per capita income change/'closures' in West Bank and Gaza, 1994–2001**

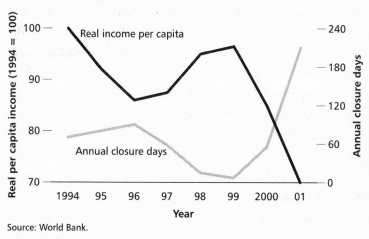

Source: World Bank.

both sides was as eager as in the case of land sales a couple of generations earlier.

Israel, it emerged, could not easily do without Palestinian labour. Nor could the Palestinians do without access to the Israeli labour market. One of the main reasons for the dramatic fall in the Palestinian GNP during the second intifada was the 'closures', the choking-off of Palestinian access to jobs in Israel by denial of passage through security checkpoints (see Figure 7). Before the outbreak of the second intifada, 130,000 Palestinians worked in Israel – of whom about half were clandestine workers without permits.[54] According to World Bank estimates, Palestinian GNP of roughly $5 billion before the intifada exceeded GDP by about $1 billion. This difference was primarily due to worker remittances from Palestinians employed in Israel. In other words, nearly a fifth of total Palestinian national income was derived from this source. The ripple effects went even further. In June 2001 the World Bank estimated that total closure of the Israeli labour market against Palestinians would 'imply a reduction in economic activity within the West Bank and Gaza of approximately 50 per cent'.[55] In the event, the closures were not total: after the first few weeks of the intifada and until the events of March 2002, about fifty thousand workers were de facto able to return to work in Israel and the settlements, although border crossing points were closed and reopened on many occasions.

The second intifada nevertheless wrought immense economic damage to Palestinians, as is clear from a further World Bank report issued in March 2002, that is before the large-scale Israeli incursions into the West Bank at the end of the month. The report estimated that per capita real income of Palestinians declined by 12 per cent in 2000 and by a further 19 per cent in 2001. It suggested that per capita real income in the West Bank and Gaza was then 30 per cent below the level at the time of the signature of the 'Gaza–Jericho' agreement in 1994. After that report was issued matters deteriorated further.[56] Total Palestinian GNP, which had been above $5 billion in 1999, was reduced, on an optimistic estimate, to no more than $4 billion in 2002.

By mid-2002 45 per cent of the labour force was unemployed.[57] Restrictions on labour movement were by no means the only cause. The Palestinian territories, like Israel, suffered from the collapse of tourism. The Palestinian Authority, with a bloated labour force of 122,000 people, a figure that did not include local government employees, was bankrupt and unable to pay its employees regularly. The Palestinian economy was almost paralysed by restrictions on movement of goods and the refusal by Israel after December 2000 to transfer to the PA funds collected by the Israeli tax administration, mainly VAT, purchase taxes and import duties that, under the Oslo agreements, accrue to the PA. These untransferred funds included 75 per cent of income taxes and 100 per cent of health fees paid by Palestinian workers in Israel – of course, only by officially recognized workers. (Limited transfers resumed in late 2002.) But the single most important proximate cause of the Palestinian economic crisis was undoubtedly the dramatic fall in employment remittances by Palestinians working in Israel. By late 2002 much of the Palestinian population was living in penury, on the edge of survival, reduced to reliance on subsistence farming, odd jobs, peddling, or prostitution.

The Israeli economy also suffered. Israel was hard hit after September 2000 by the collapse of tourism, by a savage downturn in the technology sector, and by a recession in the diamond industry, three of Israel's biggest foreign-currency earners. Over the next two years the country endured one of the worst recessions in its history. Foreign investment dwindled. The value of the shekel declined. Unemployment in early 2002 was recorded at an all-time high of 10.6 per cent – but this figure probably concealed a larger body of unreported unemployment.

Why, at a time of such high unemployment, does the Israeli economy retain a significant degree of dependence on imported labour? The reasons are as much social as economic. In sociological terms, or rather in terms of the social objectives of Zionism, Israel is peculiarly vulnerable to the effects of recession, since these may diminish Jewish immigration and lead to an exodus of highly skilled Jewish labour. Israeli policy-makers thus face a perplexing dilemma. They need economic growth, both for intrinsic reasons and to preserve the single element in the original Zionist dream that still holds meaning for them after all else is gone, namely the Jewishness of the state. But if such growth is to resume, Israel, like the EU, the USA, and other economies with adverse demographic prospects, needs imported labour – in Israel's case of a kind that will not compromise the Jewish majority in the state. (The example of the EU over the past decade shows, by the way, that this need can co-exist with a high level of indigenous unemployment. The reasons, which may have to do with specialization of skills and with welfare provision, need not detain us here.)

For some types of employment, labour can be geographically 'out-sourced' by means of industrial parks outside Israel's borders. Some Israeli employers have indeed begun establishing such enterprises in the Palestinian territories and further afield. But in the main sectors of Palestinian employment in Israel, namely construction, agriculture, and tourism, the nature of the work requires its performance *in situ*. Israel's only possible recourse, it would appear, is a resumption of large-scale employment of commuting labour from Palestine – just as an end to the 'closures' is the only short- to medium-term hope for a revival or even the survival of the Palestinian economy.

Partly as a counterweight to dependence on a Palestinian 'labour reserve army', Israel began in the 1990s to import foreign workers on short-term contracts. As in the case of Palestinians, these workers were attractive to Israeli employers because of their lower wages and minimal social-benefit costs. According to the Bank of Israel, the cost of employing foreigners in agriculture and construction was 40 per cent less than that of employing Israelis.[58] Eager recruits flooded in from Romania, Thailand, the CIS, Turkey, Ghana, Malaysia, the Philippines, and even China – which alone sent 11,600 such workers to Israel in 2001.[59] Theoretically, these entered for a year or so at a time before returning home. But Israel, like many other countries, found that short-term guest-workers evolved almost imperceptibly into long-term residents. Many remained illegally. Others found ways and means of doing so legally. Some married Israeli Jews or Arabs, established families, and put down roots. Some parts of southern Tel Aviv, for example Neve Sha'anan, Hatikva, and the Carmel Market districts, were transformed into ethnic enclaves of such workers with distinctive characteristics, social customs, and institutions such as churches and social-service organizations – and brothels catering to the many single young men among this population. By the end of the decade 'white flight' of Israelis from such areas was becoming discernible. Official figures indicated there were 95,000 foreign workers in Israel at the end of 2001. In addition, an estimated 141,000 so-called 'visa over-stayers' remained in the country as of October 2001.[60]

In December 2001 the Labour and Social Affairs Ministry banned any further entry of temporary foreign workers. But unofficial arrivals continued, generally of people purporting to be tourists. According to a report in early 2002, 40 per cent of so-called 'legal' aliens had been in the country for six or more years.[61] In May Israeli police announced that 300 Chinese had stolen in using the same underground route used by prostitutes from Egypt. The following August the government announced that it would immediately deport 50,000 illegal aliens. But in spite of official efforts to stem the flow, the influx of foreign labour continued inexorably. In November 2002 the Bank of Israel estimated the number present in the country had risen to 262,000, of whom two-thirds did not hold work permits.[62]

The increasing fuzziness of lines of national demarcation in Israel is exemplified by the appearance of this new group that is neither Jewish nor Arab. That is quite apart from an-other non-Jewish and non-Arab component of the popula-tion – immigrants entering the country under the Law of Return who are not practising or self-identifying Jews, though they may be of partly Jewish descent or have Jewish family members. In recent years, an outright majority of all immigrants to Israel under the Law of Return, particularly from the CIS and Ethiopia, have been non-Jews. Thus a law designed to provide a refuge to persecuted Jews and to for-tify the Jewish character of Israel has unexpectedly become an avenue for economic migration of non-Jews to Israel.

This development has compelled the Israel Central Bureau of Statistics and other government departments to revise their categories for disaggregating the population. The Ministry of Interior, for example, defined 108,000 persons in 1999 as 'religion unclassified'. The CBI reported about 270,000 non-Jewish residents of Israel at the end of that year (leaving aside Arabs and Druzes). They are the most rapidly growing social group in Israel today and, counted together with supposedly temporary foreign workers, probably number altogether around half a million.

One indication of the changes in collective social identity arising from this group's presence was the decision of the Knesset in 2002 to eliminate the category of 'nationality' (*le'om*) from Israeli identity cards, though it will be retained, for the time being, on the Interior Ministry's population register. Another is the pressure from several directions towards facilitating conversion to Judaism of non-Jewish immigrants from the CIS and Ethiopia, for example the Falash Mura – a group claiming descent from Falashas (Ethiopian Jews) forcibly converted to Christianity several generations ago.

Until the 1970s conversion to Judaism in Israel was rare and difficult. The orthodox rabbinical establishment maintained its monopoly control of such conversions and, as in the Diaspora, tended to put obstacles in the way of applicants. The start of large-scale Jewish immigration from the Soviet Union in 1971 inaugurated a gradual change. In many cases so-called 'quickie conversions' were arranged for non-Jewish family members of immigrants either en route in Europe or after arrival in Israel. In spite of their general disapproval of such practices, the rabbinical courts turned a blind eye, mindful of the danger that if they did not sanction them, others, in particular the mainly American Reform and Conservative Judaism movements, might use the issue as a wedge to challenge the orthodox monopoly in Israel. Mass immigration from the Soviet Union from 1988 onwards brought the issue to a head. In an important test case in 1995, the Supreme Court ordered the Ministry of Interior to recognize a conversion that had been conducted in Israel under Reform Jewish auspices. Under pressure from orthodox religious parties in the ruling coalition to push through legislation that would deny state recognition to conversions performed in Israel under non-orthodox auspices, the Netanyahu government in 1997 set up a committee to recommend guidelines for non-orthodox conversions. The committee proposed the creation of 'conversion institutes' that would prepare applicants and would operate in a manner satisfactory to all three denominations: the actual conversions would be performed under orthodox auspices. Such conversions were not recognized by ultra-orthodox groups. But the number of conversions nevertheless grew rapidly from 1,531 in 1996 to 4,130 in 1999.[63]

The growth of the third element in the population arouses even greater concern among some Israeli leaders than dependence on Arab labour. Orthodox Jews conducted a powerful rearguard resistance. In 1998 the Interior Ministry ordered Russian immigrants whose Jewish ancestry was in question to undergo DNA tests that would supposedly confirm their Jewishness.[64] In 1999 the Minister for Diaspora Jewish Affairs, Michael Melchior, called the phenomenon 'a ticking time bomb'.[65] Melchior, although an orthodox rabbi, is a political 'dove'. For him, as for other Israeli leaders, steering between foreign and Palestinian labour is as perilous as Ulysses' course between Scylla and Charybdis. But whatever route is taken, the destination is not a homogeneous or hermetically separate Jewish Israeli society but rather a pluralistic one in a relatively open relationship with its surroundings and with the world. This represents an evolution and perhaps a mutation in the society's value system. By some that may be seen as a betrayal of the fundamental ideals of the founders of Zionism. By others it may be interpreted rather as a realization and vindication of core elements within those ideals.

3 Environment

All national movements assert a special relationship to the land that they claim. Zionism, because it did not yet occupy the land, went further: it intended to 'reclaim' the land, to restore it to productive use from what were alleged to be centuries of neglect. A hundred years of rapid development have indeed transformed the landscape of Palestine. Huge population growth, intensive agriculture, insensitive urban planning, road-building on a vast scale, and the development of an industrial economy have all wreaked havoc on the ecology of Palestine. Many species of mammals, reptiles, and migrating birds have disappeared altogether from the country. Others are on the endangered list. Most of Israel's few rivers are so polluted that fish cannot survive in them. Nor can humans: in 1997 four Australian athletes attending the Maccabiya international sports tournament were killed as they walked in procession over a bridge across the River Yarkon in Tel Aviv. The bridge collapsed. Two died of their injuries; the other two were victims of the poisons in the water.

Any country may ignore environmental constraints in the short term; no country can do so in the long term. Middle Eastern states in general have displayed a reckless disregard for the consequences of their extraction of natural resources. Israel's record is no worse than that of any of her neighbours

– but her land area and potential for such exploitation are much more limited than those of most other states in the region. Palestinians have not had sovereign control of their environment and their pace of economic development has been much slower than that of Israel. Yet in the Palestinian territories, as in Israel, pressure of growing population on the natural environment has reached crisis point.

As the number of residents has grown, so, inevitably, has population density. In 1922 Palestine held just thirty people per sq. km. By 2001 Israel, with 294 people per sq. km within the 'green line', was one of the most densely populated countries in the world. In the West Bank in the same year, density was 342 persons per sq. km. For comparison, Lebanon had a density of 314 while the Netherlands, the most densely populated country in Europe, recorded a level of 372. But neither Lebanon nor the Netherlands includes a large area of desert. The Southern District of Israel, containing the Negev desert (also some cities such as Beersheba), had a density per sq. km of just 65 persons. By contrast, the figure for the Gaza Strip was 2,933 and for the Tel Aviv area 6,788.[1] The coastal plain region, constituting no more than a fifth of the land area of Israel, contains nearly two-thirds of its population (see Map 4). The urban sprawl around Tel Aviv is now such that Israelis talk of the 'Los Angelization' of the region.

The re-afforestation of the barren hillsides of Palestine loomed large in the Zionist imagination. In 1905 the Zionist Organization decided to commemorate its recently deceased founder, Theodor Herzl, by planting a forest in his

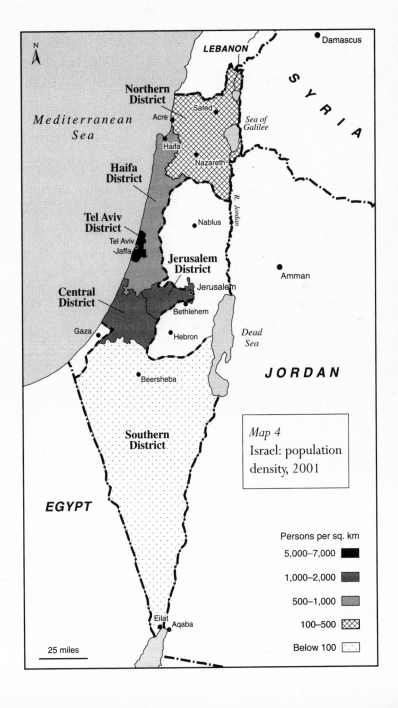

N

Mediterranean Sea

LEBANON

Damascus

S Y R I A

Northern District

Safed

Acre

Sea of Galilee

Haifa

Nazareth

Haifa District

Tel Aviv District

Tel Aviv -Jaffa

Nablus

R. Jordan

Jerusalem District

Jerusalem

Amman

Central District

Bethlehem

Gaza

Hebron

Dead Sea

J O R D A N

Beersheba

Southern District

Map 4
Israel: population density, 2001

EGYPT

Eilat

Aqaba

25 miles

Persons per sq. km

5,000–7,000

1,000–2,000

500–1,000

100–500

Below 100

name. To this end an Olive Tree Fund (*Ölbaumspende*) was inaugurated.[2] It gave rise to one of Zionism's most popular and successful fund-raising campaigns. Throughout the Diaspora, donations for tree-planting were collected in ubiquitous Jewish National Fund (JNF) 'blue boxes', particularly on the New Year for Trees, a traditional holiday that was lent a new nationalist coloration. Individual trees were planted in children's names, groves dedicated in honour of communal worthies, and donors of whole forests were inscribed in a 'Golden Book'. In the Zionist historical narrative, the Jewish devotion to trees, in both ancient and modern times, was contrasted with the attitude of 'the Arab conquerors' who had 'ravaged' the forests.[3] A process of forest destruction indeed appears to have taken place in the late Ottoman period, particularly during the First World War. The mandatory government did not even form a Department of Forests until 1936. In the later years of the mandate the government planted about 800,000 trees a year and private bodies, notably the JNF, a further 600,000. Between 1960 and 2001 the total afforested area (excluding natural forests) in Israel tripled. Altogether, in the course of the twentieth century the JNF claimed to have planted 220 million trees.

Yet the vision of Israel as a Levantine Norway was not realized. Israel remained one of the least afforested countries on the Mediterranean littoral. By 1996 only 3.7 per cent of Israel was covered by forest, compared, for example, with 7 per cent in Lebanon and 8 per cent in Morocco.[4] Moreover, some of the imported species of tree that were planted, in an apparent effort to Europeanize the landscape prospect, turned out to be highly susceptible to disease and fire.

Among Palestinians too, trees occupied a significant place in popular thought. Some, especially carobs and black fig trees, were said to be haunted by *djinns* (demons). Others, including specific oaks, terebinths, and olive trees, were traditionally considered the habitations of Muslim saints. In many cases, individual 'holy trees' were held to testify to the former 'forest glory' of Palestine.[5] Such trees were considered immune to the depredations of locusts. A few had quasi-nationalistic significance – for example, Sittnah al-Gharah, the 'Laurel Lady', situated east of Beit Nuba, near Latrun. According to legend, 'the Laurel Lady appeared during the attack of the British (1917), standing on top of the tree, with a greenish garment, a light head-shawl and a sword in her hand, which dripped with blood. Every time the English troops advanced, she threw them back.'[6] Some Christian Arabs too attributed sanctity to particular trees, for example olive trees in the Garden of Gethsemane in Jerusalem and in the 'Shepherd's Field' near Bethlehem. In post-1948 Palestinian Arabic literature of exile, trees, particularly olive and lemon trees, often assumed a symbolic importance as reminders of a lost, paradisiac homeland.[7]

In the West Bank the hillsides remained generally bare of trees. Under Jordanian rule little afforestation was carried out, save in the Jenin area. Meanwhile many naturally forested areas were depleted by Palestinian peasants for fuel. The ravages of climate and of flocks further reduced the number of trees. In 1997 forested tracts in the West Bank were estimated to comprise no more than 0.89 per cent of the total area. Palestinians complained that many areas even of these limited resources were being uprooted to make way for Jewish settlements.[8]

Given the centrality of trees in Zionist ideology and in Palestinian folklore, it is not surprising that they became objects of conflict. In Palestine, as elsewhere around the Mediterranean (notably Greece and Algeria) in the twentieth century, destructive burning of trees became a common form of political protest. From the 1920s onwards accusations were heard that Arabs were committing arson against Jewish-planted forests. During the early years of the first intifada it was estimated that one-third of all forest fires in the country were caused by arson, generally committed on nationalist grounds. Palestinians were said to be fighting an 'environmental intifada'. During the second intifada the tables were turned. Now Jewish settlers attacked Arab-owned olive groves in the West Bank, destroying trees and preventing landowners from gathering fruit. And the Israeli army razed orchards of their trees, particularly in the Gaza Strip, in order to create 'free-fire' zones.

No less vital than afforestation to Zionism's conception of its task was the 'harnessing' of Palestine's water resources. Water has played a prominent role in the history of the Arab–Israeli conflict from the outset. During and after the Paris Peace Conference in 1919, the Zionists pressed hard to ensure that the sources of the Jordan fell within the British, rather than the French, mandated area. They strongly supported the application of Pinhas Rutenberg, a former Russian revolutionary turned Zionist, for a concession to utilize the Jordan waters for the production of hydro-electricity. When activated, the concession made a major contribution to the electrification of the country.

During the mandatory period rapid Zionist development led to the frequent sinking of unauthorized wells and to British administrative counter-efforts that were as ineffective as the government's attempts to limit Jewish land purchase. Zionist interests, such as the Mekorot water company, successfully resisted passage of an ordinance that would have enabled the government to control the exploitation of underground water resources. As the government's Water Commissioner noted sadly in 1944, in a memorandum on over-pumping in the Haifa area, 'I have no powers to sanction or prohibit the sinking of wells to tap the underground water sources. Until we have powers to control the exploitation of the underground sources of water, private companies and owners will continue to sink wells as and where they please, irrespective of the danger of depleting and ruining valuable underground reservoirs and irrespective of the rights of other users.'[9] Although wartime defence regulations gave officials the right to intervene, in practice they found themselves unable to control the sinking of new wells. By 1946, the Water Commissioner was in despair over continued over-pumping in the Haifa area: 'The situation is now much worse and disaster is in sight.'[10]

In the 1948 war, Iraqi troops seized the Jerusalem water source at Ras al-Ain and, until they were ejected by Israeli forces, reduced the supply of besieged west Jerusalem to a trickle. After the establishment of Israel water became a strategic and diplomatic issue that periodically threatened to bring the country to blows with its neighbours. In 1967, for example, conflict over the Jordan waters played a significant part in the descent to war. And in 2002 Lebanese plans to divert one of the sources of the Jordan prompted a warning of military action from the Israeli government.

The supremacy of development over conservation in Zionist thinking had particularly deleterious results in relation to Palestine's water resources. Palestine holds only three large bodies of inland water: the Dead Sea, Lake Huleh and the Sea of Galilee (Lake Tiberias). All have suffered severely as a result of misconceived policies. The most serious case is the Dead Sea, currently bordered by Israel and Jordan. The lowest place on the surface of the earth and one of the natural wonders of the world, this salt lake has been subjected to savage environmental degradation over recent decades. Reduced water flow from the River Jordan and rapacious mineral extraction by both the Israeli and the Jordanian phosphate industries have produced a steady lowering of the water level – from about 1,280 feet below sea level in 1930 to 1,360 feet below sea level in 1999. In the same period the shoreline has receded by more than fifty yards. Israel's Water Commissioner was unrepentant when questioned in 1999 about the consequences for this unique lake: 'Instead of feeding the Dead Sea, let's revive a dead desert,' he said.[11] Substantial investment has been made in tourist facilities on the western shore of the sea. But already several years ago the visitor was confronted not with one Dead Sea but two, since the drop in level had led to the emergence of a natural cause-way across it. Today the entire southern end of the sea has virtually dried up. The length of the sea from its northern to its southern tip has shrunk from 75 to 55 km. The water level is now said to be declining by about three feet per annum. At that rate the entire sea could be dry by 2050. Meanwhile the accelerating death of the sea is destroying the fragile eco-systems around its shores.

Several proposals have been put forward for replenish-ment of the Dead Sea. In 1890 a Swiss engineer, Max Bour-cart, suggested the construction of a canal from the Mediterranean. The idea was revived in the 1940s and 1950s by the American agronomist Walter Lowdermilk who de-vised a grandiose scheme for a 'Med–Dead' canal that would refill the sea with salt water and at the same time generate hydro-electricity.[12] Such a plan received initial approval from the Israeli government in the 1980s – but was never realized. More recently, at the world environment summit in Johan-nesburg in 2002, the Israeli and Jordanian Environment Ministers signed an agreement for the joint construction of a pipeline to bring sea water from the Red Sea to the Dead Sea. The pact was unaccompanied by any allocation of fund-ing for a project that was estimated to cost a billion dollars. But if implemented, 'Red–Dead', like 'Med–Dead', threat-ened serious environmental damage, in this case to the Arava desert south of the Dead Sea as well as to the natural ecolog-ical balance in and around the sea.

The case of the 'reclamation' of the Huleh swamps illus-trates the potentially counter-productive results of highly intrusive development policies, when implemented without due consideration of environmental consequences. In the late nineteenth century Lake Huleh, situated on the River Jordan, north of the Sea of Galilee (see Map 5), occupied an area of 12–14 sq. km and was surrounded by a further 48 sq. km of marshland. The Reverend George Adam Smith, author of *The Historical Geography of the Holy Land* (a learned and influential product of nineteenth-century biblical scholarship), wrote of the area: 'Once, probably, it was all a lake. Today this has shrunk to its lower end, the so-called Lake of Huleh, and the rest is marsh and fat meadow, with a few mounds and terraces covered by trees.' He added: 'The lake might easily be drained; almost as easily it might be extended, as it seems to have been, to the limits of the plain.'[13] In the early twentieth century the lake is said to have boasted 'the richest diversity of aquatic biota in the Levant ... [including] 260 species of insects, 95 crustaceans, 30 snails and clams, 21 fishes, seven amphibians and reptiles, 131 birds and three mammals'.[14] But the area was infested with malarial mosquitoes, rendering human habitation difficult.

The first scheme for reclamation of the region was conceived in the 1860s by a visiting Scotsman. On the eve of the First World War two Beirut merchants were granted a concession by the Ottoman government for drainage of the swamps. Realization of the project was delayed by the war and then by legal and other difficulties. The area was purchased by the Jewish-controlled Palestine Land Development Company in 1934 and a new drainage concession was granted by the government. But the outbreak of the Arab

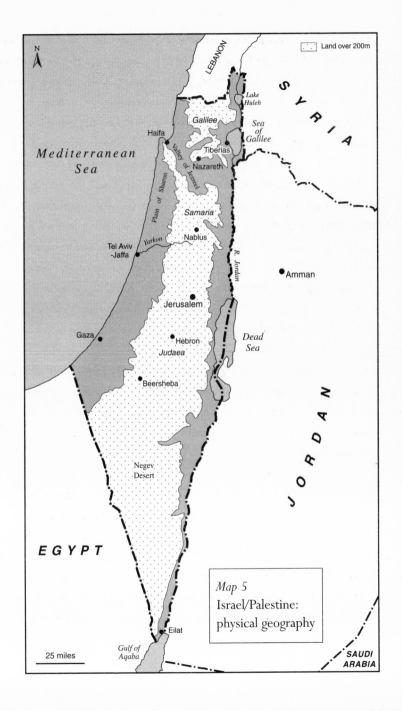

Map 5
Israel/Palestine:
physical geography

revolt and then the Second World War once again prevented the work being undertaken. It was not until 1950 that drainage finally began. In the first stage, 800 Arab villagers were compulsorily removed from their homes in the area. By 1958 12,350 acres of swampland around the lake had been drained and turned into arable land to be cultivated by Jewish settlers. Malaria was entirely eliminated from the district. The project was hailed as a great achievement of Zionist development and tourists were taken to witness the seemingly miraculous transformation that had been wrought in the landscape.

But the drastic artificial change in the eco-system of the region had unexpected and untoward consequences. The groundwater table fell. The soil turned to dust. As the earth dried, the population of field mice soared and the rodents devoured crops. Farmers abandoned the area. Decomposing peat from the drained area released great quantities of nitrates that were carried by the Jordan into the Sea of Galilee, adversely affecting its water quality. Large numbers of plant and animal species were lost. By the 1980s the project was acknowledged to have been a costly failure. In 1994, in an effort to restore a natural ecological balance, part of the 're-claimed' area was re-flooded and named Lake Agmon.

Israel's third body of water, the Sea of Galilee, is by far the most important since it constitutes Israel's main fresh-water reservoir. In recent years its level has steadily declined and in 2001 fell to a record low point, 215 metres below sea level. Inflow from the northern reaches of the Jordan was also the lowest ever recorded. Meanwhile the salinity level rose to

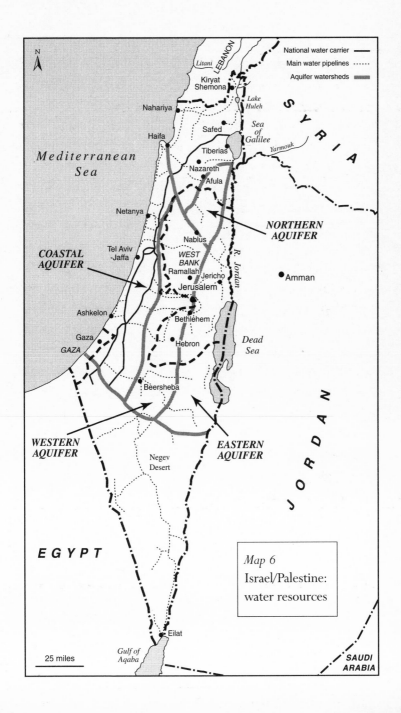

N

Litani LEBANON

Kiryat
Shemona

Nahariya   Lake
                  Huleh

          Safed   Sea
Haifa   of
                  Galilee

          Tiberias   Yarmouk

Mediterranean   Nazareth
Sea   Afula

                          S Y R I A

Netanya   *NORTHERN
                                AQUIFER*

              Nablus
COASTAL   *WEST*
AQUIFER Tel Aviv *BANK*
           -Jaffa Ramallah Jericho
                   Jerusalem
                              R. Jordan
                                      ● Amman

Ashkelon   Bethlehem

Gaza   Hebron   Dead
GAZA   Sea

              Beersheba
                                      J O R D A N
WESTERN
AQUIFER   Negev   *EASTERN*
                  Desert   *AQUIFER*

E G Y P T

                          Map 6
                          Israel/Palestine:
                          water resources

25 miles   Eilat
            Gulf of
            Aqaba   *SAUDI*
                                ARABIA

National water carrier ——
Main water pipelines ------
Aquifer watersheds   ▨▨▨

292 mg of chlorine per litre, well above the 250 mg recommended ceiling for drinking water.[15] The main reason was over-pumping from the lake into the Israeli National Water Carrier, a large network of waterways completed in 1964 (see Map 6). Other contributory factors were a run of dry years and growing Lebanese abstraction of water from the sources of the River Jordan above its inflow to the lake.

Israel resorted to several expedients to deal with the problem. One was an ostrich-like bureaucratic redefinition of the 'red line', the lower limit set for the lake. Until 1981 this was set at 212 metres below sea level and no pumping was permitted once that was neared. Since then, the line has been lowered on four occasions, most recently in 2001 when it was set at minus 214.25 metres. But even that level was breached shortly afterwards and the Water Authority seemed to have abandoned the concept of a 'red line' altogether. Evidently other measures were required. But what should a rational water policy for Israel look like – and how would that impinge upon political relations with Israel's neighbours?

Public thinking, and therefore political policy-making, about water in the Middle East in general and Israel/Palestine in particular is largely shaped by mythology – often related to nationalistic totems. Perhaps no other aspect of the Israeli–Palestinian relationship is so replete with popular misconceptions. For example, contrary to a widespread notion, precipitation in much of Palestine is not low by comparison with most European countries (Jerusalem's average annual rainfall of about 600 mm is higher than that of London, Paris, Berlin or Warsaw). Eric Mills noted in 1931 that it was 'remarkable that with a constant annual rainfall of volume roughly equal to that of the rainfall of eastern England there have been in the history of the country few permanent constructions for the conservation of water. It is not untrue to say that the history of Palestine is to be interpreted in terms of a failure to conserve its supply of water.'[16]

In the early years of Zionism it was generally – and fallaciously – believed that water was not merely one among many vital resources but the essential condition for and constraint upon economic development. For example in 1946, in their economic survey of Palestine entitled *Palestine: Problem and Promise*, Nathan, Gass, and Creamer wrote: 'Water supply is at present the most important natural limitation on the ability of Palestine to absorb large numbers of new immigrants.'[17] Irrigation had certainly played an important role in the development of intensive agriculture by the Zionists in the mandatory period – though by 1947 only 8 per cent of all cultivated land in the country was irrigated. But, as we have seen, the majority of Jewish immigrants settled in towns and worked in economic sectors much less heavily dependent on water. Today it is still commonly believed in Israel and Palestine that water is a critical strategic issue, that a growing population must necessarily devour ever-greater quantities of it, and that competition for an increasingly scarce supply is likely to lead to exacerbated conflict.

Many of the implicit assumptions on which such fears are based are questionable. First of all, contrary to popular wisdom, growing populations and economies do not necessarily and invariably require parallel increment of water supply.

The reverse is closer to reality: advanced industrial economies need less water than primitive agrarian ones. According to one authority, water in industries and services can produce *ten thousand* times the economic returns of water used in irrigation.[18] In the United States, water consumption declined between 1980 and 1995 from 1,900 gallons per person per annum to about 1,500, according to the US Geological Survey. This was during a period of rapid population growth and economic expansion. And the trend there is continuing.[19]

Hydrologists tell us that, as a region, the Middle East ran out of water in the 1970s and Israel/Palestine ran out in the 1950s – if by 'running out' we mean lacking sufficient water to meet total needs, industrial, municipal, household, and, most critically, for food production.[20] Yet an illuminating study by J. A. Allan, *The Middle East Water Question*, denies that the area necessarily faces a water catastrophe. Allan argues that 'water resources do not determine socio-economic development: socio-economic development determines water management options'.[21] Water, he points out, has come to have a symbolic as well as an economic value in many societies. Israel, he writes, is the only Middle Eastern economy that has 'adopted comprehensively the principles of demand management' in relation to water, this despite 'its enduring, if somewhat "invented", traditions of a rural and water intensive way of life'. These traditions, he notes, 'are still held sacred by a majority of Israelis' and he recalls that Israeli reliance on water beneath the West Bank is sometimes cited as a justification for continuing to hold strategic territory. Yet,

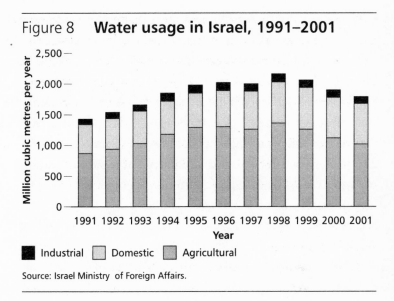

Figure 8   **Water usage in Israel, 1991–2001**

Source: Israel Ministry of Foreign Affairs.

according to Allan, the Israeli case demonstrates that the development of a diverse modern industrial economy can submerge deeply held traditional views on water and much else.[22] Far from facing an imminent disaster, he argues, Israel offers a model of effective water management. In Israel, as elsewhere, the overwhelming bulk of water is consumed by agriculture (see Figure 8). Yet agriculture today, as we have noted, contributes only 2 per cent of Israeli GDP. The solution is plain: cut water consumption in agriculture.

Israel has, in fact, done that. The influence of agricultural pressure groups has diminished in recent decades as a result of the decline of the kibbutzim (moshavim and private farmers have always exercised less political leverage) and the end of Labour's hegemonic role in the political system.

Accordingly, Israeli governments have had more leeway to take decisions on water issues that might be resisted by agriculture. Private ownership of water resources in Israel was abolished by the Water Law of 1959 and the Water Commissioner, appointed by the government, has sweeping powers over all water issues. Regulations issued in 1976 set out the following order of priorities in 'rationing areas' (i.e. areas where demand for water exceeded supply): (1) domestic usage; (2) industrial; (3) agricultural; (4) other. Since most of the country was classified as a 'rationing area', agricultural water needs were clearly designated as of low priority. Agricultural usage was gradually curtailed, partly by administrative action, particularly after 1986, and partly by reduction in subsidies for water used in farming. Further depletion of available supply led in 1999 to a reduction of 40 per cent in average water quotas for agriculture, and of 50 per cent in 2000–2002.[23] Israel's total water usage as a consequence declined significantly between 1998 and 2001. Cuts in water quotas have stimulated greater efficiency in the use of water by agriculture, for example the so-called 'drip irrigation' method pioneered in Israel. Overall, between 1975 and 2001 the average allocation of water to agriculture per unit of land area was reduced by more than a third while agricultural output nevertheless increased substantially.[24] Even were that not so, Allan argues, Israel could make up any shortfall in food needs by importing what he calls 'virtual water', i.e. food.

Other solutions are also being implemented or investigated. One is reuse by the agricultural sector of recycled domestic waste water. Another is desalination, the cost of which has declined substantially since the mid-1980s. According to current plans, desalinated sea water should supply 7.5 per cent of Israel's estimated water needs by 2020. A third recourse, probably in the long run the most expensive, is physical importation of sweet water by super-tanker, underwater pipeline or 'floating bags'. In 2002 Israel signed a contract with Turkey for the purchase of water, to be transported by ships – but large-scale reliance on this would be very costly: at the moment only some of the Persian Gulf statelets can afford to rely heavily on such physical importation of water. Peace with Israel's northern neighbours, however, would facilitate the realization of a long-planned project for construction of a water pipeline from Turkey to the River Litani and the sources of the River Jordan in Lebanon.

Nevertheless, even if Israel does not face an imminent water catastrophe, complacency is not in order. Over the past two decades the coastal and the inland aquifers have been depleting rapidly and the water table of the coastal one, in particular, has fallen so far that, particularly in the Gaza region, it is becoming dangerously saline. Israelis have depended increasingly on water from the inland aquifer, situated mainly below the West Bank (see Map 6). This dependence is not a product of the occupation. Even before June 1967 a quarter of Israel's water supply was drawn from wells and springs within Israel that tapped the inland aquifer; at that time this drawing represented more than ten times the Palestinian usage.[25]

Conflict over water has grown more acute in recent years and has become a significant element in the Israeli–Palestinian dispute. The Israeli occupation administration after 1967 limited Palestinian access to the aquifer by restricting permission for new wells. Moreover, many Palestinian villages remained unconnected to piped water networks and had to rely entirely on wells or on the collection of rainfall in cisterns. As a result, by the late 1990s West Bank Palestinians had one of the lowest water consumption rates in the world: 20 to 30 cubic metres per person per year.[26] Such administrative barriers to access to water probably accelerated the drift out of agriculture among Palestinians in the West Bank. By then Israelis were using five times as much water as Palestinians – this included Israeli settlers whose use of water from the inland aquifer, seen by Palestinians as a national resource, was resented, especially as settlers were charged at preferential rates. In the Gaza Strip Israeli settlers in the 1980s were accorded water quotas two or three times the size of those granted to their Palestinian neighbours. This level of allocation turned out to be insufficient for their needs and in 1986, for example, they exceeded their quota by 36 per cent.[27]

After 2000 water, like trees, became a focus of conflict in the intifada. In July 2002, for example, Israeli television reported that 'pirate' taps were being hooked up to pipelines belonging to the Israeli Mekorot water company which, under Israeli–Palestinian agreements, supplied both Israeli and Palestinian settlements in the West Bank. Israel's Water Commissioner estimated in July 2002 that the total annual quantity of water being 'stolen' by Palestinians amounted to as much as ten million cubic metres – a third of the annual quantity being supplied to the Palestinian Authority by Israel.[28] In October 2002 the Israeli Minister of Infrastructures (responsible for water), Effi Eitam, a supporter of the Jewish settler movement, accused the Palestinians of large-scale violations of agreements on water. He alleged that they were conducting a 'water intifada' against Israel by failing to build water purification facilities in the hope of polluting Israel's ground water. Eitam further complained that some 250 unauthorized water drillings had been conducted in the course of the year in areas of the West Bank under Palestinian control. In response, he ordered the Israeli National Water Commissioner to halt all drilling for well water by Palestinians in the West Bank.[29]

Yet, while competition for water has been heightened in the short term, longer-run pressures seem likely to force the two sides to cooperate. No wall can be erected between the water resources on which both Israelis and Palestinians depend. As Ron Zweig of Tel Aviv University has put it with graphic simplicity: 'Their sewage flows into our water-table; our sewage flows on to their beaches.' In 2000 Dalia Itzik, then Israeli Environment Minister, acknowledged that 40 per cent of the water piped to Israeli and Palestinian homes in 2000 was 'undrinkable'. She said the situation was 'catastrophic'.[30] In order to try to cope with the immediate problem, the Israeli Water Commission shut down some wells, operated others only for non-potable uses, and rehabilitated other water sources by the installation of desalination and purification plants.

In the longer term both Israelis and Palestinians are coming to recognize that coordination is not merely desirable; it is unavoidable. A report by a joint Israeli–Palestinian committee of hydrological experts in 1999 declared:

> In contrast to surface water, it is very difficult to divide an aquifer physically ... Moreover, aquifers are susceptible to pollution from mismanaged human activities, and to salinization if they are over-pumped. In either case, once an aquifer is degraded its storage capacity is reduced. These factors create a high level of hydrological interdependence between Palestinians and Israelis. Given this interdependence, the option of 'divorce' – a split operation whereby each side would manage it as it sees fit – cannot succeed and would inevitably lead to future conflicts.[31]

The experts therefore concluded:

> As neither side can manage the aquifer on its own, such management has to be done jointly ... If joint management is not institutionalized, crucial storage capacity and quality levels may be lost, to the detriment of future generations of both Israelis and Palestinians. Therefore the real choice the two sides face is between a lose–lose situation if they do not cooperate and a potential win–win situation if they do.[32]

Hence the effort by the two sides to reach an agreement on sharing water.

In negotiations with Israel in the 1990s the Palestinians complained bitterly that Israel was plundering what should rightly be seen as a Palestinian resource – the inland aquifer. On the other hand, since much of the Israeli extraction took place on Israeli sovereign territory, they were unable to stop it. Palestinian Authority control of large parts of the West Bank, however, opened, for the first time since 1967, the prospect of increased Palestinian tapping of the aquifer free from Israeli control. This might in the long run lead to over-drawing that would be damaging to both sides. Given continuing Israeli dependence on the inland aquifer for around a quarter of its national water supply, the Palestinians were thus able for the first time to negotiate from a position of some strength on this issue.

The Israeli–Palestinian Interim Agreement of 28 September 1995 (known as 'Oslo II') set out an agreed basis for cooperation and further negotiation on water. This opened with a statement of principle: 'Israel recognizes the Palestinian water rights in the West Bank.' Although full realization of these rights was postponed for negotiation in the permanent status agreement, practical arrangements were nevertheless concluded that settled many outstanding issues. Israel transferred to the Palestinian Authority administration of water and sewerage in the areas under its control. The two sides agreed to coordinate the management of water and sewerage resources and systems. The agreement stated that the Palestinians in the West Bank were to have access to additional water, in specified quantities and places and where necessary by new infrastructure, from the eastern branch of the inland aquifer. A Joint Water Commission as well as 'Joint Supervision and Enforcement Teams' were established to deal with all water- and sewerage-related issues in the West Bank.

During the second intifada most of the cooperative agreements between the Palestinians and Israel collapsed under the strain of the armed confrontation. Water did not, however, become a major arena of conflict. The Oslo II clause on water remained in force. And on 31 January 2001 Israel and the Palestinian Authority signed a joint declaration stating:

> The two sides wish to bring to public attention
> that the Palestinian and Israeli water and
> wastewater infrastructure is mostly intertwined
> and serves both populations. Any damage to such
> systems will harm both Palestinians and Jews ...
> We call on the general public not to damage in
> any way the water infrastructure ... [and] not to
> harm in any way the professional teams that
> conduct regular maintenance or repair damage
> and malfunctions to the water and wastewater
> infrastructure.[33]

The Israeli–Palestinian Joint Technical Committee on water and sewerage, in which American representatives also participated, continued to function through the intifada. In the course of the Israeli offensive in the West Bank in the spring and summer of 2002, Israel occasionally reduced or shut off the water supply to Palestinian towns. Military operations frequently prevented or delayed the repair of damaged pumping stations or pipelines. Nevertheless, in August 2002 the Israeli Foreign Ministry stated that dialogue with the Palestinians on environmental issues such as toxic waste, waste disposal, and pest control on the everyday level was 'very good' – though it added that 'long-term cooperation' was 'totally lacking'.[34]

What this suggests is that where competition for a resource becomes so extreme as to endanger both sides, they will recede from a 'zero-sum game' approach and instead, willy-nilly, decide to cooperate. Or, as the joint committee of water experts concluded in 1999: 'Where water is concerned, Israelis and Palestinians can be viewed as Siamese twins – two entities sharing a vital resource.'[35] Here, then, we have another illustration of the interdependence of Israeli and Palestinian societies and of the literally porous frontier between them.

4 Territory

Countries, like religions and nations, are artefacts. They and their borders are defined by humans, not by any external agency. So-called 'natural' boundaries are simply the superimposition of human assumptions on geographical features. There is no state in the world whose borders are precisely fixed by nature. Even island nations such as Ireland and Japan have difficulty securing universal recognition of their territorial self-definition – as the Irish Republic has found in the case of Northern Ireland and Japan in respect to Sakhalin. The Himalayas are the most imposing mountainous barrier between any two countries on earth; that has not prevented China and India coming to blows over the exact line of their border in that region. In 1975 Iran and Iraq signed a treaty recognizing the *thalweg* or mid-stream of the Shatt al-'Arab as the border between them; yet disputes over its exact location dragged on and contributed to the outbreak of war between the two countries in 1980.

As a political entity, there was no Palestine between ancient times and the early twentieth century. Even as an administrative unit, it did not exist before the British arrived at the end of the First World War. Under Turkish rule between 1516 and 1917/18, the Holy Land was divided into a number of administrative districts (see Map 7). The process by

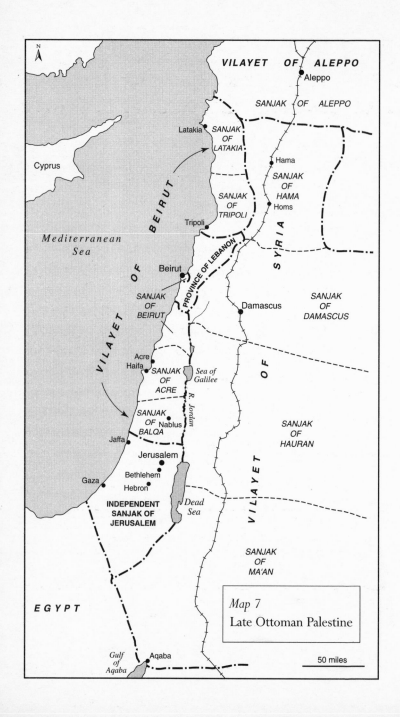

N

VILAYET OF ALEPPO

Aleppo

SANJAK OF ALEPPO

Latakia

SANJAK OF LATAKIA

Hama

SANJAK OF HAMA

Homs

SANJAK OF TRIPOLI

Tripoli

Cyprus

Mediterranean Sea

VILAYET OF BEIRUT

Beirut

PROVINCE OF LEBANON

SANJAK OF BEIRUT

Damascus

SANJAK OF DAMASCUS

SYRIA

Acre
Haifa

SANJAK OF ACRE

Sea of Galilee

R. Jordan

SANJAK OF BALQA

Nablus

Jaffa

Jerusalem

Bethlehem

Gaza

Hebron

Dead Sea

INDEPENDENT SANJAK OF JERUSALEM

SANJAK OF HAURAN

VILAYET OF

SANJAK OF MA'AN

EGYPT

Map 7
Late Ottoman Palestine

50 miles

Gulf of Aqaba

Aqaba

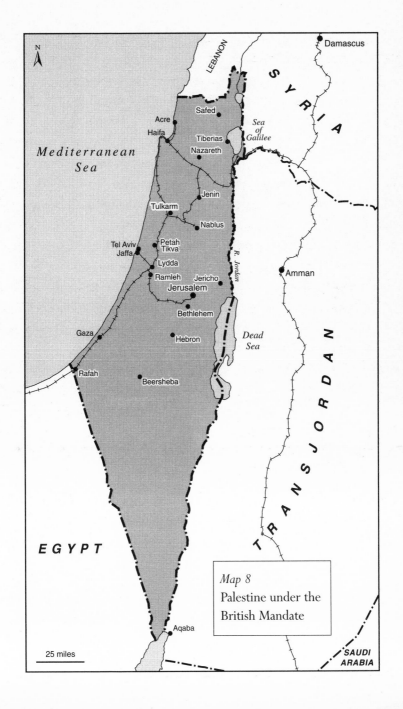

Map 8
Palestine under the
British Mandate

which Palestine's borders were established after the First World War has been the object of another exercise in nationalist myth-making (see Map 8). It is commonly stated that in 1921–2 Britain partitioned Palestine and lopped off Transjordan, thus reducing the area to which the Balfour Declaration applied to only 22 per cent of its original extent. For example, we are told: 'In 1922 Great Britain unilaterally and illegally split off 78 per cent of Palestine – all of Palestine east of the Jordan River – and gave it to Abdullah, the non-Palestinian son of the Sharif Husayn of Mecca.'[1] Since (the argument often proceeds) 78 per cent of the land area of 'historic Palestine' was illegitimately taken away from the Zionists in the supposed partition of 1922, they should not be required to yield yet more of the remaining 22 per cent. Such arguments and percentages have a mesmeric attraction for propagandists. It is now common for Palestinian nationalists to argue that 78 per cent (note the identical percentage) of mandatory Palestine (i.e. Palestine west of the River Jordan) was illegitimately appropriated by Israel in the 1947–8 war and that they should therefore not be required to yield yet more of the remaining 22 per cent.[2] At their final encounter at the Camp David summit in 2000, Yasir Arafat told President Clinton: 'You say the Israelis moved forward, but they are the *occupiers*. They are not being generous – they are not giving from their pockets but from *our* land. I am only asking that UN Resolution 242 be implemented. I am speaking only about 22 per cent of Palestine, Mr President.'[3] Another example, right down to the percentages claimed, of the copy-cat tendency of the two nationalisms.

Was Palestine partitioned in 1921–2? The text of the Balfour Declaration of 2 November 1917 refers to 'Palestine' but nowhere defines its limits. When Britain occupied the country in the course of the following eleven months, she established a military occupation regime for the whole of the Levant, under overall British control, and divided it, like Gaul, into three parts: Occupied Enemy Territory (OETA) North, the former sanjak of Beirut, covering much of what is today Lebanon, was placed under French military rule; OETA East, consisting of the districts of Damascus and Hauran, corresponding more or less to modern Syria, was placed under an Arab administration headed by the Emir Faisal; and OETA South, the former sanjaks of Acre and Nablus and the independent sanjak of Jerusalem, roughly what became British mandatory Palestine, was placed under direct British military rule.

Until 1923, when an Anglo-French convention settled the northern borders of Palestine and a conclusive peace treaty was signed with Turkey, the question of the future northern and eastern boundaries of the country and of the Jewish National Home remained open. (The Egypt–Palestine border had been agreed before the First World War.) At the Paris Peace Conference in 1919 the Zionists pressed hard for the inclusion in Palestine of the sources of the River Jordan in southern Lebanon. They also urged that the eastern border of the country be set east of the river so as to include a 25-mile wide strip of territory in Transjordan. The most forceful exponent of the Zionist proposal was the future British High Commissioner, Herbert Samuel, at that time working

closely with the Zionist Organization. In a letter to the Foreign Office in June 1919, Samuel stressed that 'for the maintenance of a population in Palestine numerous enough to
support the structure of a modern state, the fertile territory
east of the Jordan proposed to be included within the
boundaries is also essential'.[4] The Zionists received some influential support. Balfour, for example, wrote:

> In determining the Palestinian frontiers, the
> main thing to keep in mind is to make a Zionist
> policy possible by giving the fullest scope to
> economic development in Palestine. Thus the
> Northern frontier should give to Palestine a full
> command of the water power which
> geographically belongs to Palestine and not to
> Syria; while the Eastern frontier should be so
> drawn as to give the widest scope to agricultural
> development on the left bank of the Jordan,
> consistent with leaving the Hedjaz railway [which
> ran north–south about thirty miles east of the
> Jordan] completely in Arab possession.[5]

Yet in spite of this powerful advocacy, no decision on the
issue was taken at that stage.

In April 1920, when the San Remo Conference assigned
the mandate for Palestine to Great Britain, the question of
borders was raised in discussions among the members of the
Supreme Council (consisting of delegates of the USA, the
British Empire, France, Italy, and Japan). The British and

French debated the issue acrimoniously. The British Prime Minister, David Lloyd George, referred delegates to 'the ablest book on Palestine which had ever been written', George Adam Smith's *Historical Geography of the Holy Land*. In a telegram to the Foreign Office summarizing the conclusions of the conference, the Foreign Secretary, Lord Curzon, stated: 'The boundaries will not be defined in Peace Treaty but are to be determined at a later date by principal Allied Powers.'[6] When Samuel set up the civil mandatory government in mid-1920 he was explicitly instructed by Curzon that his jurisdiction did not include Transjordan. Following the French occupation of Damascus in July 1920, the French, acting in accordance with their wartime agreements with Britain, refrained from extending their rule south into Transjordan. That autumn Emir Faisal's brother, Abdullah, led a band of armed men north from the Hedjaz into Transjordan and threatened to attack Syria and vindicate the Hashemites' right to overlordship there. Samuel seized the opportunity to press the case for British control. He succeeded. In March 1921 the Colonial Secretary, Winston Churchill, visited the Middle East and endorsed an arrangement whereby Transjordan would be added to the Palestine mandate, with Abdullah as its Emir under the authority of the High Commissioner, and with the condition that the Jewish National Home provisions of the Palestine mandate would not apply there.

Palestine, therefore, was not partitioned in 1921–2. Transjordan was not excised but, on the contrary, added on to the mandatory area. Zionism was barred from seeking to expand there – but the Balfour Declaration had never previously applied to the area east of the Jordan. Why is this important? Because the myth of Palestine's 'first partition' has become part of the concept of 'Greater Israel' and of the ideology of Jabotinsky's Revisionist Zionist movement. Long after the establishment of Israel, the Revisionists' political heirs, the Herut Party (the core element in what became the Likud) led by Menahem Begin, still dreamed of a Jewish state that would include Transjordan. Their catch-phrase was 'The Jordan has two banks: one is ours and the other too!' Most Revisionists conveniently forgot that their ideological hero, Jabotinsky, had, as a member of the Zionist Executive, endorsed the arrangements in 1922 that explicitly prohibited Jewish settlement in Transjordan. More recently, advocates of Israeli annexation of the West Bank have asserted that the proper home of the Palestinian Arabs is in Transjordan: hence the slogan 'Jordan is Palestine'.

The creation of Transjordan, then, has nothing to do with partition, properly understood, save for the purposes of some propagandists. Yet the origins of the partition of Palestine are to be found in the early 1920s. The concept of partition did not appear suddenly when President George W. Bush began talking about a 'two-state' solution in 2002, nor out of the UN General Assembly resolution of 29 November 1947, nor out of the Palestine Royal Commission Report of 1937 which first recommended it officially. It was not merely a product either of diplomacy or of war.

The origins of partition lay in Herbert Samuel's failure in the early 1920s to create a unified political community in

Palestine embracing both Jews and Arabs. The collapse of his efforts to construct a constitutional government with joint Arab–Jewish political institutions, in particular a legislative council, paved the way, *faute de mieux*, for a process of internal, institutional partition. The Jewish Agency, an umbrella for the Zionist Organization, was set up to represent the Jews and exercised a growing degree of autonomous control over the *Yishuv*. And the Supreme Muslim Council, headed by the Mufti of Jerusalem, Hajj Amin al-Husayni, performed what was in some respects an analogous role vis-à-vis the Muslims. Gradually, during the 1920s and early 1930s, these two bodies developed into what have been called quasi-governments of the Jews and the Arabs in Palestine. Thus, long before any question arose of territorial partition, the mandatory government had laid the groundwork for it by means of policies that institutionalized the social and economic lines of division between Arabs and Jews.

This already existing institutional partition provided one of the justifications for the geographical partition proposed by the Royal Commission in 1937. Its key recommendation was the partition of Palestine into a small Jewish state, a larger Arab state linked to Transjordan, and a residual British mandatory area stretching from Jerusalem to the sea and including Lydda and Ramleh, as well as Nazareth, the Sea of Galilee, Tiberias, Safed, Haifa, and Acre (see Map 9). Partition was rejected by the Arab nationalists. As for the Zionists, it was strenuously opposed by the Revisionist movement, by the Mizrahi (religious Zionists), by some General Zionists (followers of Weizmann), and by sections of

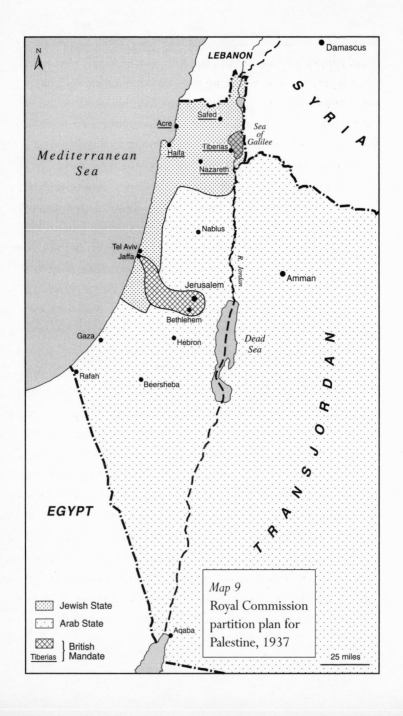

Map 9
Royal Commission
partition plan for
Palestine, 1937

Jewish State
Arar State
British Mandate
Tiberias

25 miles

the Labour Zionist movement (dominant in the *Yishuv*). It was supported, at least in principle, by the two most imposing figures in the movement, Weizmann and Ben-Gurion, and eventually by a majority at the Zionist Congress which demanded, however, substantial enlargement of the proposed area of the Jewish state.

Under the Commission's proposals, the Jewish state would cover only a small part of the country, although the Jews would acquire the great bulk of the most productive agricultural land. The Commission's recommendations were primarily based on the existing distribution of Jewish land ownership and population. Since the early 1930s, the Zionists had been buying land strategically with the object of building large contiguous blocks of Jewish-owned land, particularly in the coastal plain, the *Emek* (the Valley of Jezreel), and the upper reaches of the River Jordan. The geographical distribution of Jewish-owned land (see Map 2) demonstrates the relationship between Jewish land ownership and the Commission's territorial recommendations.

The other main element in determining the Commission's border recommendations was population distribution. Their proposals would have created an Arab state with a minority of 1,250 Jews. But the Jewish state would have had a minority of at least 225,000 Arabs – only slightly short of the initial Jewish population, though, of course, that would be expected to increase rapidly as a result of large-scale immigration. The Commission therefore made a second, even more radical recommendation: it proposed what it called an 'exchange of land and population' whereby the small Jewish minority in the Arab state might be moved to the Jewish state and the large Arab minority in the Jewish state would be moved to the Arab state, including Transjordan. It envisaged an agreement, similar to that between the Greeks and the Turks in 1923, and, as in that case, it suggested that 'it should be part of the agreement that in the last resort the exchange would be compulsory'.[7]

Benny Morris has argued that the idea of 'transfer' of Arabs from Palestine to Transjordan or beyond had a much longer pedigree and a much greater salience in Zionist thinking than most previous Israeli historians have acknowledged. He quotes Israel Zangwill's famous remark in 1905 that the Arabs should 'fold their tents and silently steal away'; Ruppin's proposal in 1911 for 'a limited population transfer'; Weizmann's suggestion in 1930 that a 'quasi-exchange of population could be fostered and encouraged'; and Ben-Gurion's statement to the Zionist Congress in 1937: 'Transfer ... is what will make possible a comprehensive settlement programme'; as well as similar statements by other representative figures from various sections of the Zionist movement.[8] Other historians such as Neil Caplan, Anita Shapira, Yosef Gorni, and Nur Masalha have all discussed this issue within the larger context of evolving Zionist attitudes towards the so-called 'Arab problem' in Palestine and have reached varying conclusions. Perhaps Morris stretches things a little when he writes that transfer was 'one of the main currents in Zionist ideology from the movement's inception'. But it was certainly a significant current and the government's approval in principle of the

Royal Commission's proposals marked a decisive shift in British official thinking.

One of the most trenchant critiques of the Commission's proposals, from the Zionist point of view, was written by the former Political Secretary of the Zionist Organization, Leonard Stein, in a memorandum in August 1937. In words that have considerable contemporary relevance, he pointed out

> the derisory area of the Jewish State; its
> vulnerable frontiers; the cutting-off of Jerusalem;
> the temporary mandates over Haifa and three
> other towns; the setting-up of a Jewish state thus
> excluding more than one-third of the present
> Jewish population, and including, on the other
> hand, a population consisting as to nearly one-
> half Arabs; the handing-over of the Negev, the
> Dead Sea Mineral works, and the main works of
> the Palestine Electric Corporation to an Arab
> State.[9]

Substitute 'Arab' for 'Jewish' and vice versa in that passage and you come close to some of the chief objections that were expressed after the Camp David conference of 2000 to the proposals presented there by Israel for a Palestinian state.

Stein continued:

> As to the proposed transfer of population, it
> seems clear that, even on the most optimistic

view, it is highly improbable that any such
transfer will in practice be capable of being
carried out on the scale or at the pace
contemplated by the Peel report. If it is not
carried out rapidly and on a large scale, it will
leave the Jewish State with a minority problem of
the most formidable dimensions. If it is carried
out rapidly and on a large scale, then, whether
the Jewish State is formally responsible or not,
the odium attaching to the swift and wholesale
evacuation of Arab peasants from their homes
will fall mainly on the Jews, with results which
will be embarrassing not only to the Jewish State
itself, but to Jews in other parts of the world.
The odium will be all the greater because,
notwithstanding the euphemisms employed by
the Royal Commission, it will in fact be a case of
unilateral transfer and not of 'exchange'.

A prophetic utterance.

Although the British government initially endorsed the
principle of partition, it rapidly got cold feet, particularly
about the proposals for compulsory population transfer. A
memorandum by Eric Mills in December 1937 drew attention to some of the difficulties from the British viewpoint.
He argued that 'to give effect to these proposals is, first, to
check a natural movement relieving pressure of population
in the hill-country; and, secondly, greatly to increase the
pressure of population in that region'. Given the small

proportion of unworked land in the maritime plain that might yet be brought into cultivation, and given the fact that Jews were switching much faster than Arabs from extensive to intensive agriculture, Mills predicted:

> After the uncultivated lands in Jewish ownership
> have been occupied, the Jews in the Jewish State
> will naturally seek to displace Arabs since the
> process of 'packing Arabs closer together' by
> means of intensive agriculture will be too slow
> for Jewish needs.

Mills considered as remote the possibilities for expanding the cultivable area in the hill regions that would form the greater part of the projected Arab state and he was similarly doubtful about the prospects of introducing intensive agriculture there. As a result, he argued, development in the Arab state would 'not keep pace with the development of the Jewish enterprise in the Jewish State'. Given his similar pessimism about settlement prospects in Transjordan and the Negev, Mills concluded:

> If settlement in those areas is not practicable,
> and if the population to be transferred cannot
> find subsistence in the hills, as appears to be the
> inference from this analysis, the proposals for the
> compulsory transfer of the Arab population from
> the Jewish State cannot be brought into effect.
> Indeed, if migration from the hill-country in the

> Arab State to the Jewish State is not permitted,
> there is ground for supposing that the livelihood
> of the next generation in the hill-country will be
> precarious.[10]

No doubt partly in view of such considerations but mainly because of fierce Arab hostility to the scheme, the government formally abandoned partition in 1938. Yet partition, and even transfer of population, remained on the agenda for long-range British planning and resurfaced during the war in secret ministerial discussions on the future of the country.

Land acquisition and population distribution were not the only ways in which the future contours of the Jewish state began to take shape long before 1948. The administration of Palestine in the 1930s too foreshadowed ethnic partition. From quite early on in the mandate, and particularly after 1936, there was an inclination to assign Jewish officials to posts where they would deal mainly with the Jewish population and similarly to assign Arab officials to areas where they would deal mainly with the Arab population. The practice was not universal but it became common, particularly in the district administration. This tendency was reflected also in the delineation of administrative districts, although, for political reasons, this was rarely acknowledged.

In 1939, for example, the government reorganized the administration of Palestine, announcing that its objective was 'a division of the country into areas having a predominantly urban population and areas having a predominantly rural population'.[11] Given the disparity between the Jewish and

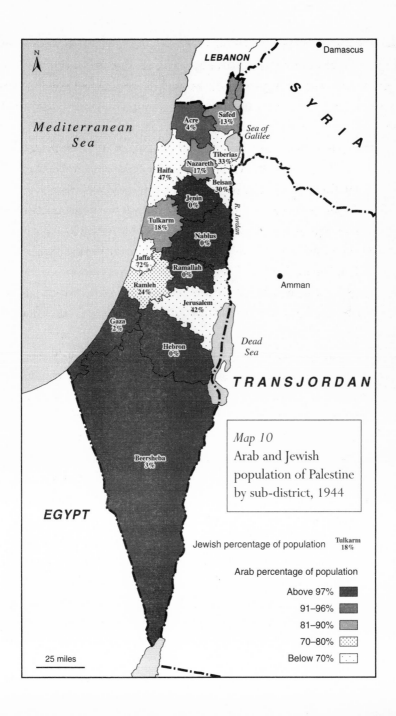

Map 10
Arab and Jewish
population of Palestine
by sub-district, 1944

LEBANON

Damascus

SYRIA

Mediterranean
Sea

Acre
4%

Safed
13%

Sea of
Galilee

Tiberias
33%

Nazareth
17%

Beisan
30%

Haifa
47%

Jenin
0%

R. Jordan

Tulkarm
18%

Nablus
0%

Jaffa
72%

Ramallah
0%

Ramleh
24%

Amman

Jerusalem
42%

Gaza
2%

Dead
Sea

Hebron
0%

TRANSJORDAN

Beersheba
3%

EGYPT

Jewish percentage of population
Tulkarm
18%

Arab percentage of population

Above 97%

91–96%

81–90%

70–80%

Below 70%

25 miles

Arab rates of urbanization, this was in itself a disguised form of proto-partition (see map 10). The changes led to a Zionist complaint that the Southern District was to be renamed the 'Lydda District'. The Jewish Agency pointed out that the population had a 60/40 Jewish majority over Arabs, was predominantly urban, and included the city of Tel Aviv, which accounted for more than a third of the district's inhabitants. The Agency found it 'difficult to see how the object of bringing out the predominantly urban character of the district in question is to be achieved by using as its designation the name of a small and relatively insignificant semi-rural township comprising only 2% of the district's population'.[12] Of course, the real offence in the eyes of the Zionists was not the size of Lydda but rather the fact that it was an Arab, not a Jewish, town.

The government held to its position but the Jewish Agency continued to press the point. In 1945 official guidance was issued to the government-run Palestine Broadcasting Service for use in reply to a listener who had submitted a question on the subject to the *Citizen Wants to Know* series on the wireless. After what appears to have been considerable research, the government suggested that the PBS announcer should read out the following ingenious (though far from ingenuous) reply:

> This question seems to reflect a measure of
> surprise which is itself a little surprising. In the
> British way of thinking it does not appear to be
> in the least inconsistent to name an

administrative division after one of its less
populous centres. The ten largest cities in
England are found in counties named after
relatively small towns. No less than four of these
ten cities are in Yorkshire – Sheffield, Leeds,
Hull and Bradford – but the county takes its
name from the old minster city of York. The
second city in England – industrial Birmingham
– is in Warwickshire with Warwick itself neatly
tucked away in the shadow of a great mediaeval
castle. In Scotland, the little town of Lanark
sleeps round the statue of William Wallace in
orchards while thirty miles away, in the largest
city in Lanarkshire, Glasgow's 1¼ million
inhabitants bustle through the clangour of its
factories and engineering shops. There seemed
nothing incongruous, accordingly, in calling an
administrative division in Palestine after Lydda –
the birthplace of St George, patron Saint of
England; nor did this small favour to the
Mandatory seem too great a favour to ask of the
people of Palestine.[13]

A different kind of problem arose relating to Jewish rural
areas in predominantly Arab districts. For example, the Jewish Agency protested after the Haifa and Samaria District
was split in two. The Agency pointed out 'that one result of
the new division will be that an important zone of Jewish settlement will find itself included in a district administered

from a purely Arab town which is surrounded by an entirely Arab area'. Alluding to the prevalent lack of security on account of the Arab revolt, the Agency argued that it was 'inconceivable, in present circumstances, that Jews should proceed to Nablus on administrative business or that the Government should appoint Jewish officials at Nablus to assist the District Commissioner in handling affairs of Jewish interest'. The Agency therefore urged an adjustment of the district boundaries.[14] The problem was solved by the government with a neat form of localized quasi-partition. The Jewish-inhabited areas remained in the Tulkarm sub-district under the charge of a Jewish District Officer stationed at Netanya. A Jewish medical officer regularly visited the area from Haifa and the District Engineer in Haifa was in charge of public works. In 1941 the Assistant District Commissioner recommended that district offices should incorporate revenue offices. If that were done, he pointed out, 'the Jewish settlements will, for all practical purposes, be a Sub-District on their own though without territorial boundaries'.[15]

The UN Special Committee on Palestine, in its proposed partition borders in 1947, had regard to the same criteria as earlier British planners, in particular distribution of population and land ownership. They deliberately eschewed strategic considerations, instead creating a criss-cross territorial arrangement with 'kissing points' between the proposed Arab and Jewish states that would, in the judgement of the committee, compel the two to cooperate. The General Assembly made some adjustments to the committee's proposals but the final UN plan, as approved in November 1947,

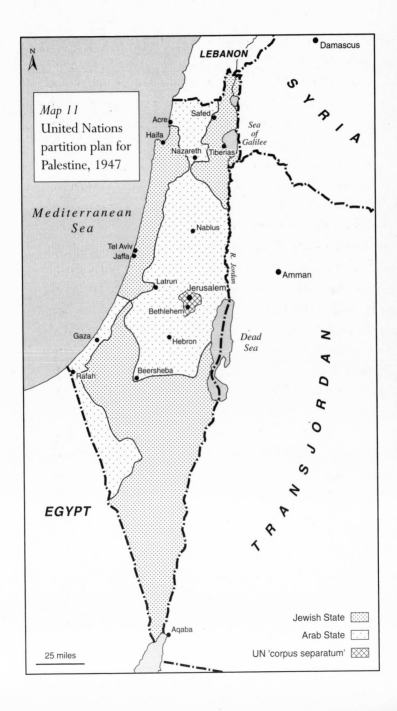

N

Map 11
United Nations
partition plan for
Palestine, 1947

LEBANON

• Damascus

S Y R I A

Acre •
Safed •
Sea of Galilee

Haifa •

Nazareth •
Tiberias •

Mediterranean
Sea

Nablus •

Tel Aviv •
Jaffa •

R. Jordan

Latrun •
Jerusalem
Bethlehem •

• Amman

Hebron •

Dead Sea

Gaza •

Beersheba •

Rafah •

EGYPT

T R A N S J O R D A N

Aqaba •

25 miles

Jewish State

Arab State

UN 'corpus separatum'

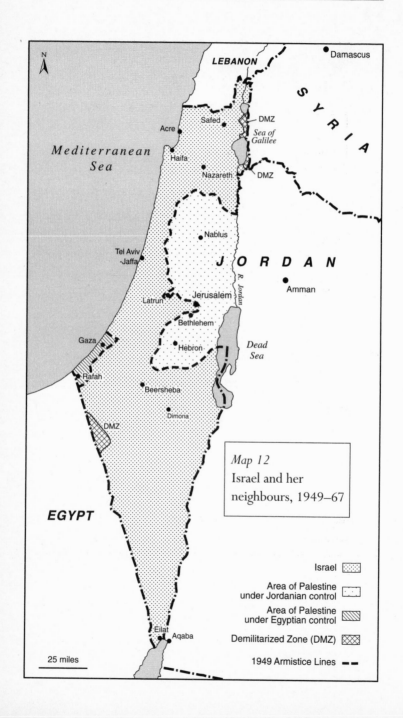

Map 12
Israel and her
neighbours, 1949–67

Israel

Area of Palestine
under Jordanian control

Area of Palestine
under Egyptian control

Demilitarized Zone (DMZ)

1949 Armistice Lines

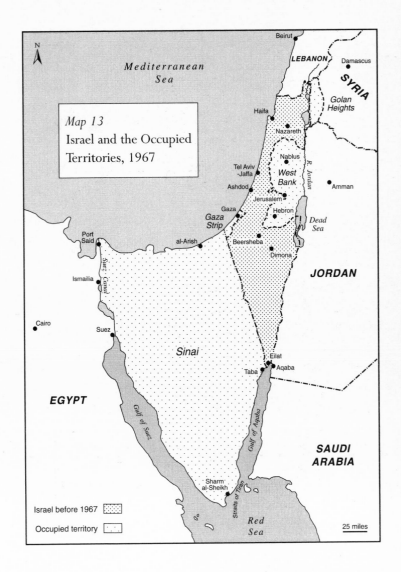

Map 13
Israel and the Occupied
Territories, 1967

Israel before 1967

Occupied territory

25 miles

retained the patchwork pattern (see Map 11). Although the UN plan provided the Jewish state with international legitimacy, Israel's borders in 1949 (see Map 12) were in the end determined by military victory. Yet their essential foundation was the demographic and socio-economic reality of the Jewish National Home as it had developed over the previous generation.

It was explicitly with this historical achievement in mind that Israeli advocates of annexation of the territories occupied in 1967 (see Map 13) sought once more to create solid Jewish demographic and socio-economic realities that would guarantee permanent Israeli control of those areas.

The 1967 Israel–Arab war thrust the question of partition on to the political agenda anew. On 19 June, a week after the end of the war, the Israeli 'National Unity' government (that included Menahem Begin) decided unanimously to offer to withdraw from Sinai and the Golan Heights in return for peace treaties with Egypt and Syria. The initiative yielded no response. From the outset, the attitude towards the West Bank was more equivocal. Israel was in any case determined at that stage to hold on to east Jerusalem.[16] In early 1968, the Prime Minister, Levi Eshkol, held a series of talks with Arab notables from the West Bank, in which he broached the idea of some form of Palestinian autonomy. But these local leaders did not dare to act independently of either Jordan or the increasingly vocal Palestine Liberation Organization.

The Palestine National Covenant of 1964 had explicitly repudiated any notion of partition. 'Palestine,' it declared, 'with the boundaries it had during the British Mandate, is an indivisible territorial unit.' (It is worth remarking that such a resolutely anti-imperialist body as the PLO thus took, as the essential basis of its ideology, frontiers that were first drawn on the map by British imperialists.) Lest there be any doubt on the subject, the Covenant added: 'The partition of Palestine in 1947 and the establishment of the state of Israel are entirely illegal, regardless of the passage of time, because they were contrary to the will of the Palestinian people and to their natural right in their homeland, and inconsistent with the principles embodied in the Charter of the United Nations, particularly the right to self-determination.'

Although still adhering to the notion of the occupied territories as a gage to be used in future negotiation with the Arab states, the Israeli government after 1967 embarked on an initially cautious settlement policy inspired by the Allon Plan (see Map 14). This proposal, first presented to the Cabinet on 27 July 1967, had considerable influence on subsequent Israeli geopolitical thinking. Yigal Allon, at the time Deputy Prime Minister, devised his partition plan with two basic principles in mind; the first was the creation of a defensive buffer zone in the Jordan rift that would counter any threat of an armoured attack on Israel from the east. The second was the rectification, from Israel's point of view, of her eastern border, in particular the incorporation of east Jerusalem, the elimination of the Latrun salient, lost to Jordan in the 1948 war, and the widening of the Jerusalem corridor. Conscious of the dangers involved in any attempted annexation of areas of large Palestinian population, the plan envisaged Palestinian autonomy in the bulk of the populated

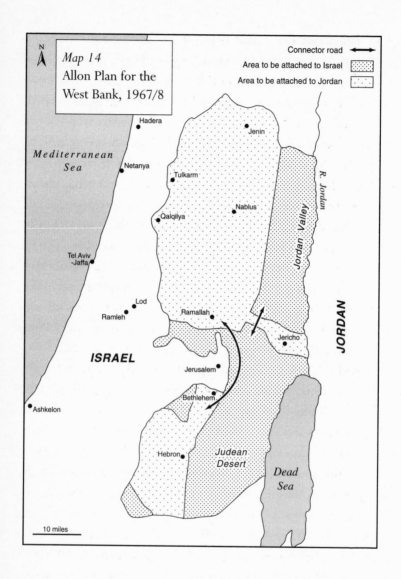

N

Map 14
Allon Plan for the
West Bank, 1967/8

Connector road
Area to be attached to Israel
Area to be attached to Jordan

Hadera

Jenin

Mediterranean
Sea

Netanya

Tulkarm

Nablus

Qalqilya

Jordan Valley

R. Jordan

Tel Aviv
-Jaffa

Lod

Ramleh

Ramallah

JORDAN

Jericho

ISRAEL

Jerusalem

Bethlehem

Ashkelon

Hebron

Judean
Desert

Dead
Sea

10 miles

hill regions of the West Bank. When it emerged that Palestinians in the area were unwilling to accept such a scheme without the imprimatur of the PLO, Allon amended his plan. The area originally earmarked for autonomy would be returned to Jordan and a land corridor linking the east and west banks of the Jordan would be added. In September 1968 Allon and the Israeli Foreign Minister, Abba Eban, met King Hussein of Jordan secretly in London and broached the plan. But the Jordanian monarch rejected it outright.

The Allon Plan nevertheless remained the basis of the Israeli government's thinking on the West Bank for the next decade. Construction of new Jewish residential districts was largely confined to east Jerusalem and areas earmarked for future Israeli annexation: the greater Jerusalem region and the Jordan valley. Apart from Jerusalem, only twenty-four settlements, with a total population of 5,000, were established in the West Bank during the first decade of the occupation, though others were set up in the Sinai peninsula and on the Golan Heights.

Nevertheless, it was during this period that a revived version of Revisionist Zionism coalesced with a religious Zionism that was suddenly galvanized by the capture of the Western Wall and the old city of Jerusalem. Messianic enthusiasts saw in these events the approach of the end of days. The two streams of thought joined in what became the Land of Israel Movement that gave rise to Gush Emunim ('Bloc of the Faithful'). From 1968 onwards a number of small groups of 'Greater Israel' devotees tried to establish settlements in the West Bank, particularly in places regarded as of religious significance. To this end the land was scoured with a view to identifying Jewish 'holy places' (although the concept had hitherto been alien to Judaism). As a result, the number of such sites mushroomed over the next few years. Hebron was a particular target of the movement, first because it was one of the four traditional holy cities of the Land of Israel (the others, Jerusalem, Safed, and Tiberias, all, apart from east Jerusalem, within pre-1967 Israel), and secondly because of the memory of the massacre of Jews there in 1929 and the eviction of the remaining Jewish community, long settled in the city. In April 1968 Rabbi Moshe Levinger, a violent religio-nationalist, and a small group of followers set themselves down in Hebron and refused to leave. The government eventually capitulated and agreed to establish a Jewish settlement, Kiryat Arba, next to the city. This fateful decision, later bitterly regretted by some, like Shimon Peres, who shared responsibility for it, set a pattern for future wildcat occupations by settler groups elsewhere in the West Bank.

After the election in 1977 of Israel's first Likud-dominated government, headed by Menahem Begin, the pace of settlement quickened (see Map 15). The policy now was mass Jewish settlement of all the occupied territories with the objective of hastening their permanent integration into Israel. The settlements were heavily subsidized by the Israeli taxpayer and a number of incentives were provided to encourage young people in particular to move to them.

Yet the growth of the Jewish settler population in the 1980s was concentrated less in the heartland of the West Bank than in those parts closest to Tel Aviv and Jerusalem.

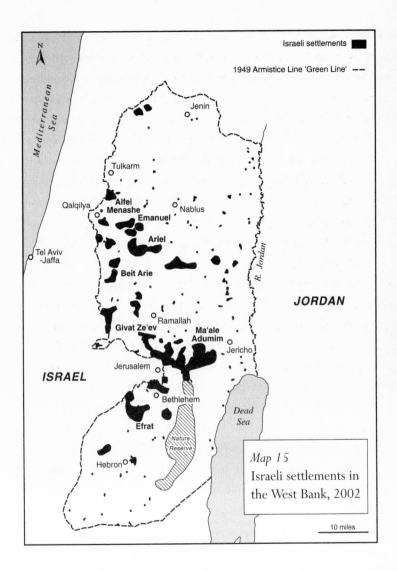

Israeli settlements ▬

1949 Armistice Line 'Green Line' ‒ ‒

Map 15
Israeli settlements in
the West Bank, 2002

10 miles

127

Rather than agricultural settlements created by ideologically driven movements such as Gush Emunim, these were suburban communities developed by commercial entrepreneurs. Their inhabitants were inspired less by nationalist motives than by an economic interest in cheap housing within easy commuting distance of the large urban centres. They were responding not to any religious injunction to settle the land but to newspaper advertisements offering inexpensive apartments 'five minutes from Kfar Saba' (an Israeli town near the 'green line' – the pre-1967 border).

The 'Oslo II' agreement between the Israelis and Palestinians in 1995 transformed the map of the West Bank into what has been called a 'cartographic cheeseboard' or a 'postmodern map, with a seemingly haphazard distribution of Palestinian and Israeli enclaves, bypass roads, and disconnected territorial nodes'[17] (see map 16). The agreement was acknowledged by both sides as an interim stage and the general presumption was that further Israeli withdrawals would lead to the creation of a Palestinian state in most of the West Bank. Nevertheless, the growth of settlements continued after the agreement which was held by the Israelis to limit only the foundation of new settlements and not 'natural growth' in existing ones. The right-wing government of Binyamin Netanyahu between 1996 and 1999 further held that the limitation on new settlements did not apply in Jerusalem and on that basis established large housing developments within the municipal boundary (as expanded after the Six-Day War). The Labour-dominated government of Ehud Barak in 1999–2001 continued settlement expansion

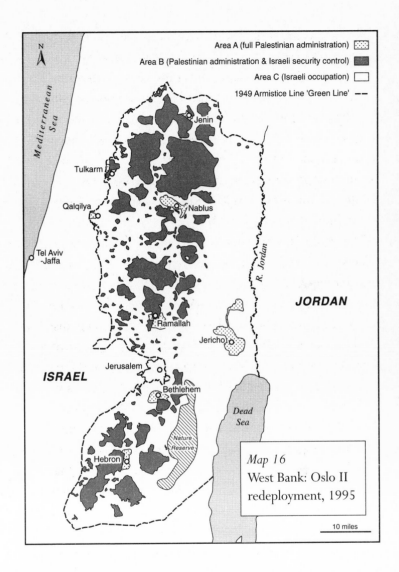

Area A (full Palestinian administration)
Area B (Palestinian administration & Israeli security control)
Area C (Israeli occupation)
1949 Armistice Line 'Green Line'

Map 16
West Bank: Oslo II
redeployment, 1995

10 miles

at breakneck speed and maintained tax and other incentives in favour of settlers.

Even after the outbreak of the second intifada the settlements continued to grow, though the rate of increase slowed. In spite of the deaths of many settlers in terrorist attacks, Jews continued to move into settlements, even those in the more remote regions of the West Bank that were widely expected to be evacuated eventually and to become part of a Palestinian state. An example was the religious settlement of Shavei Shomron ('Returners to Samaria'), north of Nablus, first set up by Gush Emunim in 1978: new residents there in 2002 included several recent immigrants from the CIS, among whom were converts to Judaism.[18] By 2002 more than 400,000 Jews lived in 126 settlements in the West Bank (including greater Jerusalem) and nineteen settlements in the Gaza Strip as well as others in the Golan Heights.

Let us put aside all our preconceptions, and ask as political realists: is it feasible in the contemporary Near East for a militarily powerful state to occupy the territory of a neighbour, implant colonies of its own citizens in defiance of economic rationality, of international law, and of international opinion, in an area notorious for political banditry, and hope to maintain such a transformed status quo indefinitely? The candid observer must report that in certain circumstances it is indeed possible. In 1974 Turkey occupied more than one-third of the territory of Cyprus. Almost all the 200,000 Greek Cypriot residents were expelled from Turkish-occupied northern Cyprus in exchange for 65,000 Turkish Cypriots from the south. A few years later a so-called Turkish Republic of Northern Cyprus was declared and over the next quarter century 100,000 'settlers', mainly peasants from Anatolia, were imported to bolster the Turkish population of the island. Turkey suffered some diplomatic inconveniences as a result and the Cyprus issue remained unresolved. The United Nations in November 2002 set out proposals for a federal state that, for the first time, offered some serious prospect of agreement. But no serious observer now proposes the return to Turkey of the bulk of the post-1974 settlers.

May Israel hope for similar success in grinding down over time opposition to her settlement effort during the same period? The Cypriot case suggests that it is not, in principle, impossible. But an examination of the main differences between the two cases, demographic, geographical, and social, leads to a different conclusion. In Cyprus there occurred a comprehensive process of what we now call ethnic cleansing. Hardly any Greeks now live in the Turkish section of the island or Turks in the Greek section. A national consensus in Turkey supported the government's policy. Nor was Turkey's settlement effort limited by demographic constraints. If anything, the contrary was the case: Turkey's rapidly growing rural population ensured that, if she wished, she could pump almost any number of settlers into the island. Although heavily dependent on Turkey and significantly poorer than the rest of the island, the Turkish section of Cyprus did not rely for its economic survival on the Greek population of the island with whom, indeed, it cut off all economic and other relations.

The contrast with the West Bank and Gaza is plain, most notably as regards demography. The overall balance of population in both the West Bank and Gaza overwhelmingly favours the Palestinians: Palestinians today still comprise more than 99 per cent of the population in the Gaza Strip and more than 90 per cent in the West Bank (leaving aside Jerusalem).

The distribution of the Jewish population in the West Bank and Gaza, however, is by no means even (see Map 15). The great majority of the settlers live either in expanded east Jerusalem (about 175,000) or in settlements that are part of what one may call greater metropolitan Jerusalem (another 73,000) or in the western-hills strip of the West Bank (about 85,000). Thus more than 80 per cent of the settlers live either in or around Jerusalem or in the western strip of the West Bank.[19] The majority of the Jewish settlements in the West Bank, even leaving aside the new Jewish suburbs of Jerusalem, are urban rather than rural in nature. Only a small minority, mainly in the Jordan valley, are primarily agricultural. Many inhabitants of the settlements, particularly around Jerusalem and in the western parts of the West Bank, commute to jobs in Israel.

The remainder of the settlements, scattered in small enclaves among large Palestinian populations, remain the chief bone of contention. In the Gaza Strip are nineteen Israeli settlements with a total population of 6,500 surrounded by a Palestinian population of one million (see Map 17). The West Bank too contains a number of such islands of Jewish settlement. Next to Jenin, population

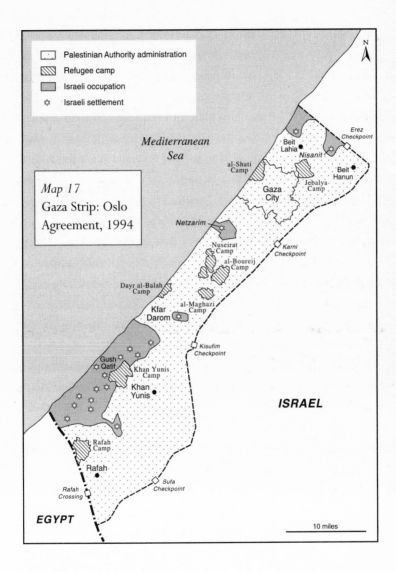

Palestinian Authority administration
Refugee camp
Israeli occupation
✡ Israeli settlement

N

Mediterranean
Sea

Map 17
Gaza Strip: Oslo
Agreement, 1994

Erez
Checkpoint

Beit
Lahia

Nisanit

al-Shati
Camp

Beit
Hanun

Gaza
City

Jebalya
Camp

Netzarim

Nuseirat
Camp

Karni
Checkpoint

al-Boureij
Camp

Dayr al-Balah
Camp

al-Maghazi
Camp

Kfar
Darom

Kisufim
Checkpoint

Gush
Qatif

Khan Yunis
Camp

Khan
Yunis

ISRAEL

Rafah
Camp

Rafah

Sufa
Checkpoint

Rafah
Crossing

EGYPT

10 miles

133

42,000, are two settlements with a total of 300 Jewish residents. Near Nablus, whose total population (including immediately adjacent villages and refugee camps) is 158,000, are Jewish settlements with fewer than 7,000 inhabitants. And in the heart of Hebron, with a population of some 140,000, is a Jewish settlement with about 400 residents. Altogether in the central hill areas of the West Bank there are about 34,000 Jews.

The 'Peace Now' movement in Israel differentiates usefully between eight types of settlements (see Table 1).

The prospects for success of the settlement enterprise depend not only on population but also on control of land and resources. In the Gaza Strip Jews, less than 1 per cent of the population, control 19 per cent of the land. The settlement of Netzarim in the northern part of the strip, with no more than fifty Israeli families, occupies as much land as the nearby Nuseirat refugee camp containing more than 60,000 people. As regards the West Bank, a report in May 2002 by the Israeli human rights organization B'Tselem stated that although the built-up areas of the settlements occupy only 1.7 per cent of the land of the West Bank, their municipal boundaries cover a total of 6.8 per cent. Moreover, the regional councils associated with the settlements cover an additional 35.1 per cent. This means, B'Tselem concludes, that the settlements effectively control no less than 41.9 per cent of the total area of the West Bank.[20] Given that an Israeli government (during and after the Camp David summit of 2000) has already laid on the table a much larger percentage of the area, the long-term outlook

Table 1 **Jewish settlements in West Bank and Gaza**

	Location	Population (Dec. 2000)
1	Gaza Strip	6,500
2	West Bank: in heart of densely populated Palestinian areas such as Hebron	18,500
3	Settlements surrounded by Palestinian villages (e.g. Elon Moreh)	16,000
4	Settlements deep in the West Bank (e.g. Ariel)	45,000
5	Settlements in the Jordan valley and near the Dead Sea	5,000
6	Settlements 'that disrupt Palestinian territorial contiguity'	20,000
7	Settlements in Gush Etzion (between Jerusalem and Hebron)	12,000
8	Settlements near the Green Line	72,000
Total		**195,000**

Source: *Ha'aretz*, 5 Dec. 2000.

for maintaining Israeli control over all the settlements must be regarded as slim.

The viability of the settlements is also a matter of security – as events since September 2000 have demonstrated. Again, Netzarim and Hebron provide poignant examples. In the first two years of the second intifada seventeen Israeli soldiers died protecting Netzarim. In Hebron, under the 1997 Israeli–Palestinian agreement regarding the city, 20 per cent of its area was retained for the time being by Israel in order to protect the 400 or so Jewish inhabitants. The Israeli-held area also contained some 30,000 Palestinians who remained subject to Israeli security control. Yet notwithstanding the large Israeli investment of military manpower and equipment in Hebron, as at Netzarim, total security was unattainable. In November 2002 three guards and nine soldiers, including the commander of Israeli forces in the city, were gunned down in an Islamic Jihad ambush near the Tomb of the Patriarchs (site of a massacre of 29 Arabs by a Jewish settler, Baruch Goldstein, in 1994).

The differences in population distribution among the settlements are, broadly speaking, inversely related to control of land area and to ideological outlook. The least populated and most isolated Jewish settlements are, in general, the ones that control the largest amount of land and that are inhabited by the most extreme nationalist groups. These are the agricultural settlements in the Gaza Strip and the hill regions of Judaea and Samaria, founded by Gush Emunim and its ilk.

So far as Gaza is concerned, the greater part of the Israeli political elite and much of the general public have come to accept in recent years that the Jewish settlements are not defensible in the long term and will sooner or later have to be vacated. In the general election campaign of January 2003 the Labour Party's platform explicitly called for evacuation of the settlements. Similarly the small Israeli population in the central-hills region of the West Bank does not appear permanently viable. These are the communities most vulnerable to abandonment by Israel in any future peace agreement or unilateral withdrawal. In contrast, the small areas of densely concentrated Jewish settlement in and around Jerusalem and on the western fringe of the West Bank appear to have the greatest prospects of remaining under permanent Israeli rule.

Israel, therefore, is probably approaching the final stages of the long secular process of territorial retraction that began after the 1973 war. Demographic, social, and economic pressures all tend in this direction. While the exact location of the Israeli–Palestinian frontier is still to be determined, that is not the only issue. No less significant is the character of that border: is it to be a porous 'Schengen'-type border, where one passes from one sovereignty to another almost without noticing it? Or will it rather be a cold-war style frontier with barbed wire fences, concrete emplacements, next to no movement of people or goods, and fortified checkpoints? Under the impact of terrorist assault, a large body of opinion in Israel today favours this type of 'iron wall' between the two peoples. But is such 'separation' feasible, given other mounting pressures on the two populations cohabiting a narrow strip of territory with limited natural resources?

5 Dynamics of political change

In August 2002 a report by Israel's National Security Council determined that the country's top security priority was 'the long-term maintenance of a firm Jewish majority and democracy'. It therefore concluded that, in light of the numerous demographic forecasts predicting an Arab majority between the Jordan River and the Mediterranean Sea, Israel must decide its final borders within the next few years and that, if no Palestinian negotiating partner were to be found, she must do so unilaterally. While the Council did not make any recommendation on the precise line of a future frontier between Israel and Palestine, it stated that Israel's borders must be fixed on the basis of 'demographic and security considerations'. The Council warned that the alternative was for Israel to retain control over an ever-growing number of Palestinians with no political rights, thereby endangering the state's Jewish and democratic characters alike.[1]

The demographic and territorial objectives that guided Zionism in its struggle with the Palestinians over the past century thus come together now, impelling Israel towards territorial compromise. Similarly, the battle between Hebrew and Arab labour in the mandatory period has given way to a common interest of both the Israeli and the Palestinian economies in an open door to Palestinian labour in Israel. And the rapid growth of both Israeli and Palestinian populations has forced both to accept the need to cooperate in their exploitation of basic natural resources such as water. Demographic, socio-economic, environmental, and territorial imperatives, therefore, all dictate an early resolution of the conflict.

Why, then, does fighting still rage? The reason is *not* that the terms of a settlement are impossible to envisage. On the contrary, the differences between the two sides over the contents of a 'permanent status' agreement have narrowed and, on some issues, are closer than ever before.

Four thorny problems still divide Israelis and Palestinians: borders, settlements, refugees, and Jerusalem.

The general contours of the future Israeli–Palestinian border are already known. It has gradually been taking shape not merely as a reflection of military and diplomatic pressures but also under the long-term influence of the demographic and socio-economic changes outlined in previous chapters. Following the outbreak of the second intifada the Oslo agreements came close to collapse: in November 2002 the newly appointed Israeli Foreign Minister, Binyamin Netanyahu, declared them 'null and void' – though this statement seemed designed more for internal political consumption in his Likud Party than as a formal statement of the government's position.[2] The agreements nevertheless retained international legitimacy. For all the heightened political rhetoric that accompanied the fighting, neither Israel nor the Palestinian Authority formally denounced the treaties and both continued to appeal (selectively) to their clauses and to demand their enforcement.

Moreover, the main political outcome of those agreements remained in effect: the Palestinian Authority continued to exist. Contrary to the hopes of some and the fears of others, it did not totally disintegrate and remained at least nominally responsible for the administration of about 40 per cent of the area of the West Bank and about 80 per cent of the Gaza Strip. In spite of their repeated military incursions into the Palestinian-administered areas, the Israelis did not show serious interest in reconstituting their military government of the West Bank and Gaza.

The present position is recognized on all sides as impermanent and the question, therefore, is what will replace it. The answer is now widely agreed: the United States, the European Union, the Arab League, the Palestinian Authority, and part of the Israeli political class all concur that an essential component in any solution is the establishment of a Palestinian state. Israeli public opinion polls since the outbreak of the intifada indicate that most Israelis expect a Palestinian state to come into being, though many of them do not relish the prospect. A poll in November 2002 found that even 52 per cent of Likud voters were willing to accept the establishment of a Palestinian state.[3] Ariel Sharon too is on record to that effect, on condition that terrorism ceases first, though his private image of such a state is probably more akin to an Indian reservation than to a genuinely sovereign polity.

The most useful starting-points for any discussion of the

Map 18
Camp David
negotiations: Israeli
proposals, 19 May 2000

Palestine
Temporary Israeli administration
To Israel

Jenin

Mediterranean Sea

Tulkarm

Qalqilya

Nablus

Tel Aviv -Jaffa

Ramallah

Jericho

ISRAEL

Jerusalem

Bethlehem

Hebron

R. Jordan

JORDAN

Dead Sea

10 miles

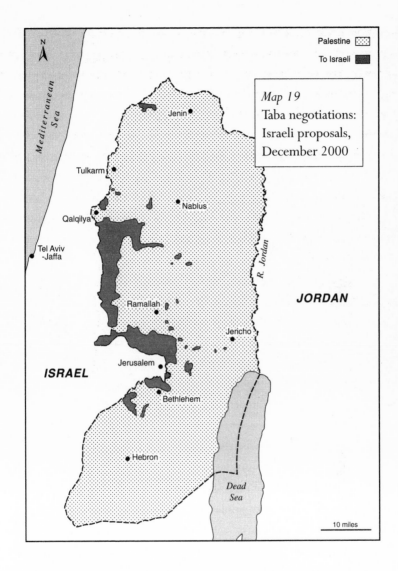

Map 19
Taba negotiations:
Israeli proposals,
December 2000

borders of a Palestinian state are the proposals that were laid on the table by Israel at Camp David in July 2000 and those submitted in the last substantive formal negotiations between Israel and the Palestinians at Taba in December 2000 (see Maps 18 and 19). A comparison of these two sets of proposals shows the extent to which, between Camp David and Taba, the Israeli position was modified in an effort to respond to Palestinian insistence on the sanctity of the 'green line' of 4 June 1967.

Since the collapse of the Camp David summit there have been a number of accounts of what occurred there, not all of them compatible.[4] But one document, drawn up by the European Union's envoy, Miguel Moratinos, claims to present an authenticated, agreed account of the conclusions of the various Israeli–Palestinian working groups at Taba in January 2001. This memorandum was leaked to the Israeli press in February 2002.[5] On Gaza Moratinos recorded that 'it was implied that the Gaza Strip will be under total Palestinian sovereignty, but details have still to be worked out. All settlements will be evacuated.' As regards the West Bank, the territorial difference between the two sides at the end of the Taba negotiations amounted to a tiny fraction of the total area. The Palestinians were prepared to yield 3.1 per cent of the territory; the Israelis proposed to retain 6 per cent, containing heavily populated settlements near the 'green line'. They were thus 2.9 per cent apart.

In order to try to resolve the difference, the two sides agreed that there might be an exchange of territory equivalent to up to 3 per cent of the West Bank, although there was

no agreement on what sovereign territory would be transferred from Israel. The Palestinians rejected Israel's proposal
that three areas should be considered part of the land swap:
the Halutza Dunes (adjacent to the Gaza Strip) in the Negev;
the area of the proposed 'safe passage' between the West
Bank and Gaza; and a section of the Israeli port of Ashdod
that would be set aside for Palestinian use.

Since Taba a new idea has surfaced in Israel, reflecting
heightened demographic anxieties. This is the suggestion by
the former Deputy Defence Minister, Ephraim Sneh, a
senior figure in the Labour Party, that some mainly Arab-
inhabited areas of Israel such as the town of Umm al-Fahm
and the so-called 'little triangle', containing more than
40,000 Arab citizens of Israel, be handed over to Palestinian
sovereignty. The proposal was given qualified endorsement
by former Prime Minister Ehud Barak: 'This could only be
done by agreement ... Such an exchange makes demographic sense and is not inconceivable.'[6] On the other hand,
the idea evoked outrage in some quarters as representing a
kind of diplomatic 'transfer' of Israeli Arab citizens to Palestinian rule. Yet the mayor of one of the towns that would be
affected, when repeatedly asked in an Israel Radio interview
in March 2002 whether he rejected the suggestion, pointedly
refused to do so. Instead, his answer was that such ideas
could be discussed only if his fellow townsfolk got back the
land that had been taken from them by the Israelis.

If the Taba negotiations offer any guide to the long-term
territorial negotiating positions of the two sides, there is sufficient basis of agreement to expect that the relatively minute

remaining differences over borders can be resolved by means of some form of territorial swap. The Moratinos document provides substantial support for the proposition that Israel would, in the final analysis, be ready to withdraw from the bulk of the occupied territories and that an agreement on borders is feasible.

Hardly less burning an issue than the location of the future border is its nature. There is a widespread feeling now in Israel, based on security considerations, that what is required is total 'separation' between Israel and Palestine in the form of an impassable physical barrier. Until recently the border between Israel and the areas controlled by the Palestinian Authority were widely seen as 'porous'. In February 2002 Ze'ev Schiff, the influential military commentator of Israel's most serious newspaper, *Ha'aretz*, pointed out that, despite all the roadblocks and closures, there were large numbers of Palestinian infiltrators in the country designated as 'illegal residents':

> These people cross the border undisturbed and
> settle in minority villages along the border. This
> involves tens of thousands of Palestinians who
> have thus realized the 'right of return' through
> the back door. But not only Palestinians
> infiltrate. With them are many Jordanians,
> Egyptians and others. Some of them get involved
> in terrorist activity and crime in Israel. From
> time to time the police conduct a manhunt and
> expel several hundred of them but they return.[7]

The main reason why so many Palestinians sought entry to Israel was undoubtedly in order to secure work in the underground labour economy, an effort in which some Israeli employers, notwithstanding security concerns, happily colluded.

To combat this phenomenon, the Israeli authorities, both left- and right-wing governments, and central as well as local administrations, resorted in the course of the 1990s to building fences. The concept of a physical barrier between Israel and the Palestinians was particularly attractive to Yitzhak Rabin, and his government between 1992 and 1995 began its construction, though in a haphazard and uncoordinated way. Ehud Barak favoured it too, declaring: 'I say the answer is separation from the Palestinians. Israel does not need or want – for security, diplomatic and moral reasons – to rule over the Palestinians. We need to separate from them physically ... "Good fences make good neighbors," as Robert Frost said.'[8]* The entire Gaza Strip was eventually surrounded by an electrified fence with adjacent free-fire zones created by the razing of citrus groves and buildings. Following the outbreak of the second intifada, Israel declared a number of areas at or near the 'green line' in the

---

*But Frost also wrote:

> Before I built a wall I'd ask to know
> What I was walling in or walling out,
> And to whom I was like to give offence.
> Something there is that doesn't love a wall,
> That wants it down.

(Mending Wall, 1915)

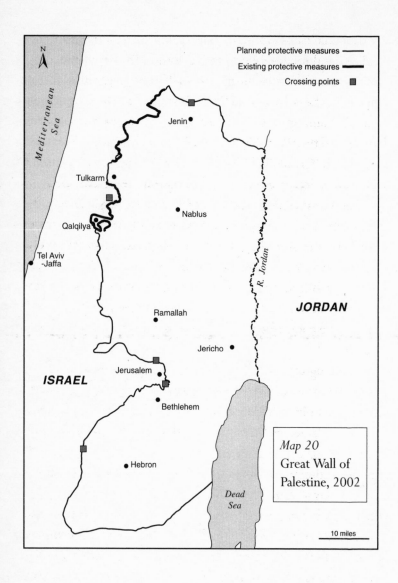

Planned protective measures ——————
Existing protective measures ——————
Crossing points ■

Mediterranean Sea

Jenin

Tulkarm

Nablus

Qalqilya

Tel Aviv
-Jaffa

R. Jordan

JORDAN

Ramallah

ISRAEL

Jericho

Jerusalem

Bethlehem

Map 20
Great Wall of
Palestine, 2002

Hebron

Dead
Sea

10 miles

West Bank 'closed military zones'. At first the fence took a localized and incomplete form: in some places it consisted of railings, in others of ditches or walls. In the spring of 2002, however, the government formally resolved to build a security barrier running close to the entire pre-1967 border between Israel and the West Bank, about 215 miles in length (see Map 20). This 'Great Wall of Palestine' would contain five crossing-points for Palestinian workers, goods and tourists.

The construction of the barrier was accompanied by the imposition of a complex new system of permits and passes for Palestinians wishing to travel into Israel or between different sections of the occupied territories. The Defence Minister, Binyamin Ben-Eliezer, stated that the objective was 'to make sure that the tens of thousands that penetrate every day to the country, that we call the unofficial workers, will be stopped'.[9]

Planning the wall led to serious internal dissension in Israel. The annexationist right opposed it, fearing that such a barrier would, in effect, delineate the future political border between Israel and a Palestinian state. Ariel Sharon, in particular, long resisted construction on this ground. The wall's construction was accompanied by official declarations that it was purely a security measure and that its location would not have any bearing on the issue of Israel's future eastern border. Both right- and left-wing elements in the government, though for different reasons, insisted on the wall's political non-significance. Nevertheless, its very existence implied recognition by the Israeli government of the continuing relevance of the 1967 border.

Once the decision to build had been taken, the government came under pressure from inhabitants of Jewish settlements near the 'green line', as well as their supporters, who demanded that the wall should not follow the old border but should deviate to the east of it so as to embrace settlements on the western edge of the West Bank. In several cases, the government yielded to this pressure, thereby storing up potential trouble in any future negotiations with the Palestinians – especially since the process often involved further expropriation of Arab-owned land.

These installations represent a large investment by Israel – though whether they will yield the desired return, in the form of enhanced security, is questionable. Israeli security authorities are divided in their views of the probable efficacy of such a barrier. No doubt it will have some effect at a local level in protecting Israelis from low-level pilfering and hooliganism – though Palestinians will remain no better protected from assault by Jewish settlers. But unless the barrier is continuous along the entire frontier, and unless passage through it by Palestinians, including Palestinian workers in Israel, is barred altogether, it is doubtful that it could be a significant deterrent to the determined terrorist.

Dubious as a security device and a monstrous environmental scar across the landscape of the country, the wall is an attempt to realize a phantasmagoric vision akin to the half-humorous desire of many Americans (before 11 September 2001) to float New York off into the Atlantic. 'Separation' represents for many left-wing Israelis a civilized alternative to 'transfer'. Yet the two concepts are really different sides of the same coin. Both rest on the illusion that Israel can, in some manner, wish the Palestinians away.

Even if Israel really needed it, resignation from the Middle East is no longer a feasible option. The reasons, as we have already seen, are economic, social, and environmental. The sealing-off of the Israeli labour market against Arab workers makes little sense for Israel. For the Palestinian economy such a permanent 'closure' would deepen the current socio-economic catastrophe. 'Separation' would also accentuate the long-term migratory trends that we have already noticed, from hill to plain and from country to town. Theoretically (and desirably in the minds of Israeli enthusiasts for 'transfer') the direction of movement might shift towards the east rather than the west. Some perceptible movement of Palestinians from the West Bank into Jordan — ostensibly 'temporary' — was reported following the outbreak of the second intifada (the same period saw the renewed appearance of posters in Israeli cities proclaiming that 'Jordan is Palestine'). But the Jordanian economy is in no condition to absorb significant numbers of poor immigrants. In an effort to staunch the flow, Jordan imposed a $1,400 caution payment, refundable on exit, on all Palestinians seeking to enter the country.[10] In the longer run, it seems much more probable that the excess population from the peripheral Palestinian regions will be drawn westwards and, in one form or another, will be sucked into the Israeli labour market. This is one major reason for doubting the durability of the new 'iron wall'. But there are others.

The kind of anti-Arab dyke envisaged by the advocates

of separation would have a gigantic hole in the middle: Jerusalem. There would only be two ways to plug that gap. The first would be to restore the wall through the middle of the holy city that existed between 1949 and 1967. But this is rejected on all sides and would hardly be feasible given the fact that 175,000 Israelis now live in the formerly Jordanian-controlled section of the city. The second way would be to build a wall around the outer edge of the current municipal boundary, thus cutting off the Arab population of east Jerusalem from the rest of the West Bank. Some Israeli political voices have been heard advocating exactly that and in some localities in Jerusalem such structures have, indeed, begun to appear. But there is a difference between local fences and an impassable security barrier. Jerusalem is the cultural, economic, touristic, and religious heart of the West Bank. To cut off the city's Palestinian population from its natural social hinterland would be to create a potentially explosive force. Far from enhancing, it would gravely undermine Israeli security.

For these and other reasons separation is unlikely to be hermetic. While security controls will, no doubt, remain so long as terrorism continues, the self-interest of both sides is likely to dictate a 'soft' border rather than a new Berlin Wall in the Middle East.

The second major issue in the conflict is Israeli settlements in the occupied territories. As we have seen, the Israeli negotiating posture at Taba clearly indicated a readiness to withdraw from all the settlements in Gaza, containing 6,500 Israelis, and from those in the Jordan valley, containing 5,400.

As for the Jordan valley, the Moratinos memorandum recorded that 'the Israeli side stated that it did not need to maintain settlements in the Jordan valley for security purposes, and its proposed maps reflected this position.' Moratinos recorded Palestinian acquiescence in Israeli annexation of some of the populous settlements on the western edge of the West Bank and Israeli acceptance that the isolated ones in the central hills would be abandoned. There remained some outstanding disagreements on the settlements, for example regarding the township of Ma'ale Adumim east of Jerusalem, but the document indicates agreement on the incorporation within Israel of a majority of the homes of Israelis living in the West Bank and east Jerusalem – though not of most of the land currently under the control of the settlers.

Of course, the government that made these proposals has fallen from power. Even when they were made, the Barak administration had lost much of its moral authority and its accredited representatives resembled the ghostly wraiths of Ottoman diplomacy who turned up at the Peace Conference in Paris in 1919 and signed the Treaty of Sèvres – the peace treaty that never was. The Taba proposals are supposedly no longer 'on the table'. But it is a well-known diplomatic principle that concessions, once proffered, are never wholly erased from memory and can therefore never be unequivocally withdrawn.

Meanwhile, the underlying demographic, social, and economic pressures (not to mention the security ones) that led to their being put on the table in the first place have not gone away. In June 2002 Ze'ev Schiff suggested that Israel

was 'approaching the stage at which it can no longer post-
pone a crucial decision on this issue [i.e. withdrawal from
isolated settlements in Gaza and the West Bank]'.[11] If anything, the pressures towards such a decision have grown
more acute since then.

It is sometimes suggested that any Israeli government that
proposed to abandon a single settlement would court civil
war and that any attempt to use the army to enforce such a
withdrawal would risk mutiny. It is true that the settlers in
some of the most isolated settlements in the West Bank include a high proportion of militant elements, among them
followers of the late Rabbi Meir Kahane and of underground
Jewish terrorist movements inspired by his racist ideology.
But such groups are indeed isolated, and not just physically,
from the mainstream of Israeli society and would be most
unlikely to succeed in mobilizing mass support for resistance
to a withdrawal decision. As for the Israeli army, in spite of
some signs of reduced morale (desertions increased significantly in 2002), it remains a disciplined, professional force
that obeys the orders of its political masters. An order to dis-
solve the settlements would be implemented. We have a
precedent for this in the case of Yamit, the Israeli-built town
in the north-east corner of Sinai, inhabited by about 2,000
people, that was evacuated in the spring of 1982 under the
terms of the Israel–Egypt Peace Treaty. Mass resistance was
promised. In the event, the army used disabling foam to
quell some settlers who tried to sit in. They were all removed
without a single serious injury. The Defence Minister responsible for overseeing the evacuation of Yamit was Ariel

Sharon. As in the case of Yamit, the settlers who leave the West Bank and Gaza will, no doubt, be offered ample compensation for their homes. Nor should the reintegration of between 40,000 and 80,000 of its own citizens represent an insurmountable challenge to a country that has, after all, absorbed much greater numbers of new immigrants in some single years since 1988.

Some advocates of Israeli annexation of the West Bank and Gaza hold that any withdrawal in the face of violence is simply an invitation to further attacks. The example of Barak's decision in 2000 to withdraw from the Israeli 'security zone' in southern Lebanon is cited in support of this contention – since the Hizbollah organization offers to the Palestinians its experience in launching attacks on Israel as a model of how to secure Israeli retreat. The annexationists' argument resembles the 'domino theory' that so impressed American supporters of the Vietnam War. It might be more persuasive if most of those who now present it had advocated withdrawal in the early years of the occupation when the pressure of violent resistance on Israel was less. Their view then was that, given the apparent acquiescence of the Palestinian population, Israel could sustain the occupation indefinitely. The case for or against withdrawal by Israel, in the final analysis, hinges not on terrorist propaganda claims but on calculation of Israeli interests. It is likely to be decided on that basis.

Even if continued Israeli occupation of the occupied territories were deemed desirable, it is not feasible without negative consequences for Israel that can only grow more acute over time. An entire civilian population cannot be kept

Figure 9 **Inter-ethnic political violence in Israel/Palestine, 1988–2001**

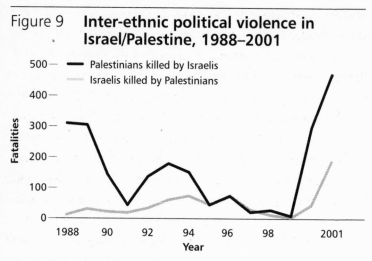

Source: B'Tselem Israeli Information Center for Human Rights in the Occupied Territories.

permanently under conditions of curfew and martial law that prevent the conduct of ordinary daily life: this is not a condition of security; it is a recipe for an explosion. A comparison between the tactics used by both sides in the first and the second intifada, suggests that both the resistance and its repression will assume ever-heightened forms of violence. The number of dead on both sides since September 2000 already far exceeds the human toll of the first intifada (see Figure 9). Continued bloodshed is likely further to undermine internal Israeli morale and external support.

The majority of Israelis do not view the preservation of the settlements as a fundamental objective of the Israeli state, nor as a contribution to its security. Nor do they equate the interests of the settlers with those of the state in general.

The likelihood, therefore, is that, sooner or later, some substantial withdrawal from the settlements will take place.

The third outstanding issue is the Palestinian refugees and their claim to a 'right of return'. The 700,000 or so refugees of 1948 have grown today, according to UNRWA, to some 3.9 million worldwide, of whom 39 per cent live in refugee camps (see Map 21). Of these, 1.6 million live in camps west of the Jordan and will become citizens of the prospective Palestinian state. A further 1.6 million live in Jordan and have been integrated into society to a considerable degree: only about 18 per cent of them still live in camps there. According to UNRWA, Syria holds 390,000 refugees, of whom 109,000 live in camps, and Lebanon 382,000, of whom 215,000 are camp-dwellers. But these figures, especially in the case of Lebanon, may well be exaggerated, both by the refugees themselves and by the Lebanese government, each for their own purposes.[12]

The Palestinian insistence at Camp David on the 'right of return' was seen by many Israelis and by some Palestinian commentators as a prime cause of the failure of the negotiations. Ehud Barak pronounced the issue to be 'existential' and insisted: 'We cannot allow even one refugee back on the basis of the "right of return". And we cannot accept historical responsibility for the problem.' Remarkably, this statement was made in the course of a cordial interview with Benny Morris, the Israeli 'new historian' who has been primarily responsible for a change in the attitude of many Israelis towards acceptance of at least partial Israeli responsibility for the Arab exodus of 1948.[13]

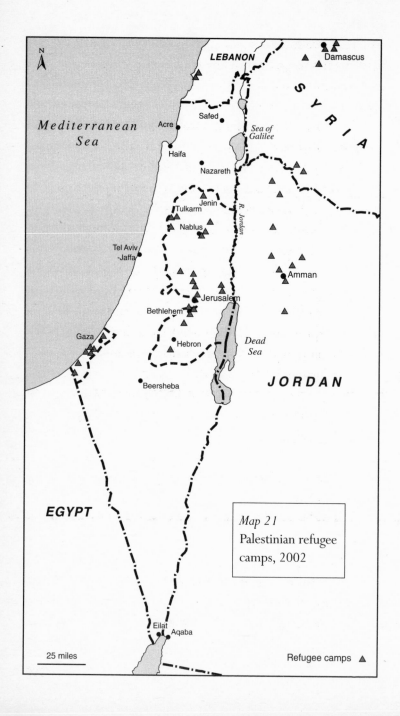

Map 21
Palestinian refugee
camps, 2002

Refugee camps ▲

The Moratinos document indicates that, even though agreement was not reached, significant progress had been made on this issue:

> The Israeli side put forward a suggested joint narrative for the tragedy of the Palestinian refugees. The Palestinian side discussed the proposed narrative and there was much progress, although no agreement was reached in an attempt to develop an historical narrative in the general text ...
>
> The Palestinian side reiterated that the Palestinian refugees should have the right of return to their homes in accordance with the interpretation of UN General Assembly Resolution 194. The Israeli side expressed its understanding that the wish to return as per wording of UNGAR194 shall be implemented within the framework of one of the following programs:
>
> A. *Return and repatriation*
> 1. to Israel
> 2. to Israel[i] swapped territory
> 3. to the Palestine state.
>
> B. *Rehabilitation and relocation*
> 1. Rehabilitation in host country.
> 2. Relocation to third country.

> Preference in all these programs shall be
> accorded to the Palestinian refugee population in
> Lebanon. The Palestinian side stressed that the
> above shall be subject to the individual free
> choice of the refugees, and shall not prejudice
> their right to return to their homes in
> accordance with its interpretation of UNGAR
> 194.

There is a general appreciation on all sides that the core of the problem is the refugees in Lebanon, whose true number is perhaps a quarter of a million. It is also understood by many in the Palestinian political class – though this under- standing has not yet been transmitted to the Palestinian gen- eral public – that most of the refugees will not go back to their former homes in what is now Israel but will instead ex- ercise their 'right of return' by moving to the Palestinian state. In an interview with Israel Army Radio in July 2001, Jibril Rajoub, then Palestinian security chief in the West Bank, said that the demand for a right of return was 'a sym- bolic demand' that was not aimed at 'calling into question the demographic balance in Israel'.[14] Sari Nusseibeh, the of- ficial Palestinian spokesman on Jerusalem until December 2002, expressed similar views in even more forceful terms and explicitly stated that the right of return should be exer- cised not in Israel but in Palestine.

Not all Palestinian politicians are so candid in their public utterances. But the 'right of return' is probably retained more as a bargaining chip and as an internal propaganda weapon than as a genuine political objective. The entire Israeli political establishment resists its implementation, seeing it as a form of Israeli political suicide; mainstream Palestinian politicians (not, of course, leaders of Hamas or other militant factions) have come, however reluctantly, to understand this and have adapted their aims accordingly.

Wrangles over the future status and disposition of Jerusalem played a central part in the discussions at Camp David and in their breakdown. But here too the two sides have narrowed down the area of disagreement. At Camp David Barak shattered a sacred Israeli political totem: for the first time since 1967 an Israeli government proposed to conduct serious discussions with a view to partial surrender of sovereignty over Jerusalem. Barak proposed that Jerusalem's boundaries be expanded to include the post-1967 Jewish settlements of Giv'at Ze'ev and Ma'ale Adumim. Some Palestinian-inhabited areas, Shu'afat, Beit Hanina and the Qalandia refugee camp, would become part of the Palestinian state. The Palestinian capital would be established at Abu Dis, near the eastern edge of Jerusalem but outside the city limits. The old city would be under Israeli sovereignty: the Jewish and Armenian quarters would be directly ruled by Israel; the Palestinians would administer the Muslim and Christian quarters. The Temple Mount (al-Haram al-Sharif) would remain Israeli sovereign territory but under day-to-day Muslim (Palestinian) control and a Palestinian flag would fly there. Jews, however, would for the first time be permitted to pray there, possibly in a designated section. The Palestinians did not move from their insistence on sovereignty over east Jerusalem, i.e. pre-1967 Jordanian Jerusalem, though they were prepared to concede the Jewish quarter of the old city.

Discussion of the Jerusalem issue continued in the Israeli–Palestinian talks held in the United States under American auspices in late 2000. In his last meeting with the negotiators from both sides, on 26 December, President Clinton proposed the 'general principle' that 'Arab areas are Palestinian and Jewish ones are Israeli'. At Taba, according to the Moratinos document,

> Both sides accepted in principle the Clinton suggestion of having a Palestinian sovereignty over Arab neighborhoods and an Israeli sovereignty over Jewish neighborhoods ...
>
> The Palestinian side understood that Israel was ready to accept Palestinian sovereignty over the Arab neighborhoods of East Jerusalem, including part of Jerusalem's Old City. The Israeli side understood that the Palestinians were ready to accept Israeli sovereignty over the Jewish Quarter of the Old City and part of the Armenian Quarter ...
>
> Both sides favored the idea of an Open City ...
>
> The Israeli side accepted that the City of Jerusalem would be the capital of the two states: Yerushalaim, capital of Israel and Al-Quds, capital of the state of Palestine. The Palestinian side expressed its only concern, namely that East

> Jerusalem is the capital of the state of Palestine ...
> Both parties have accepted the principle of
> respective control over each side's respective
> holy sites (religious control and management) ...
> Both sides agreed that the question of
> [al-]Haram al-Sharif/Temple Mount has not been
> resolved. However, both sides were close to
> accepting Clinton's ideas regarding Palestinian
> sovereignty over [al-]Haram al-Sharif
> notwithstanding Palestinian and Israeli
> reservations.

Continuing differences notwithstanding, the two sides did move closer together on Jerusalem at Taba. Ultimately, if any settlement of the issue is to be reached, the least objectionable to both sides, the Clinton formula, is likely to prevail: an open city with sovereignty divided according to the ethnic composition of districts.

As for the Temple Mount, it may be in order to recall an historical analogy – that of the conflict among the Christian sects over the Christian holy places in Palestine. No agreed solution was ever found to the endless sectarian rivalries at the Church of the Nativity in Bethlehem, the Church of the Holy Sepulchre in Jerusalem, and elsewhere. After centuries of antagonism, an exhausted acquiescence eventually emerged, based on what became the recognized principle of the status quo. This is still the governing basis for dealing with all such disputes among the rival Christian denominations. Under British mandatory rule in Palestine between

1920 and 1948, the principle was extended to non-Christian holy places such as the Western Wall. When east Jerusalem came under Israeli rule in 1967, the Israeli government implicitly accepted the status quo on the Temple Mount. The Muslim religious authorities remained in charge of the area and no Israeli government, not even that of Ariel Sharon, altered that basic policy direction. Attempts by groups of Israeli religious fanatics to assert Jewish prayer rights on the Temple Mount were firmly and repeatedly rejected by the Israeli Supreme Court, whose decisions were honoured by the Israeli authorities. The issue of sovereignty over the compound is of such paramount symbolic importance to both sides that the most likely outcome is that, as in the case of the age-old disputes over the Christian holy places, it will be left in abeyance. Meanwhile the status quo of Muslim control over the area would remain intact.[15]

If, as the Moratinos document indicates, the two sides succeeded in January 2001 in coming close to agreement on all four major issues that divided them, why has terrorism derailed the peace process, why do the two sides continue to fight with such savagery, and why has a 'permanent status' settlement not been signed? Must we conclude, after all, that Israelis and Arabs are prisoners of history, locked in unending conflict driven by ethnic, religious, or cultural attitudes so deeply ingrained as to be ineradicable?

Among both Israelis and Palestinians, religion and nationalism have joined together, for a small but significant minority, and led to an embrace with terrorism. Experts on both Judaism and Islam remind us that neither religion, historically considered, endorses such tactics. Judaism, in particular, at any rate in post-biblical times, has been, if not passive, then a demonstrably non-violent faith. The nationalist fanaticism of some contemporary orthodox rabbis and their followers is generally characterized as an aberration from and a perversion of historic Judaism. And so, indeed, it is seen by most Jews – just as most Muslims do not endorse 'Islamic terror' as a legitimate outgrowth of their faith, and just as most Christians (today) accept that anti-Semitism and persecution of 'Christ-killers' is a deformation of Christianity.

Nevertheless, given the extent to which both Israeli Jewish and Palestinian Muslim terrorists over recent decades have claimed religious legitimation for their deeds, the question arises whether there is, in fact, any sense in which their ideology has authentic religious roots. In the case of Judaism, it is too convenient to dismiss merely as twisted deformations the views expressed by orthodox rabbis such as Yitzhak Ginzburg, a member of the Habad sect (followers of the late 'Lubavitcher Rebbe', Menachem-Mendel Schneerson) and head of the government-funded 'Tomb of Joseph' Yeshiva (talmudic college) in Nablus, who declared: 'The life of Israel is worth more than the life of the gentile.' In a speech that the late Israeli political scientist and authority on Jewish terrorism Ehud Sprinzak characterized as bearing 'a seemingly fascist, almost pagan aura', Ginzburg hailed the 1994 Hebron massacre of Arabs as 'a shining moment'.[16] Ginzburg represents the outer edge of religio-nationalist extremism. Not so the former Sephardi Chief Rabbi of Israel, Ovadia

Yosef, spiritual leader of the Shas Party which won seventeen seats (out of 120) in the Knesset in the 1999 elections. In a sermon on the eve of Passover in April 2001, Yosef called for the annihilation of Arabs: 'It is forbidden to be merciful to them. You must send missiles to annihilate them. They are evil and damnable.'[17] If such views are a distortion of the 'ideal form' of Judaism, why should it be that similar statements emanate so frequently from authoritative orthodox Jewish sources?

Mutatis mutandis, similarly troubling questions are raised by the apparent religious sanction to terrorism given in pronouncements by some Muslim religious leaders, including many, such as the Mufti of Jerusalem, Sheikh Ikrema Sabri, who acclaim suicide bombers as 'martyrs' and encourage Palestinian children to risk their lives in combat against heavily armed Israeli forces.[18]

These raucous voices, whether of religio-nationalist Jewish orthodoxy or of militant political Islam, should not mislead us. They shout so loud partly because they are engaged in internal struggles on their home turf. A defensive-aggressive spirit is evident in public discourse in both the Jewish ultra-orthodox and the radical Islamic communities. Take, for example, a typical pronouncement in the Jewish ultra-orthodox weekly *Deiah ve-Dibur*:

> Those who founded a secular state for the aim of
> starting a 'New Judaism' and, *chas vesholom* [God
> forbid], annulling the Torah, are entirely unable
> to picture the Torah-observant as having any

right to exist. Someone who wants to [consign] traditional Judaism in a museum, and to protect a few remnants only as a 'historical testimony' showing what was once upon a time the Jewish Nation, is naturally not interested in further developing the Torah World, whose very existence and presence threatens the ideology of those who want a heretical state.

Perhaps this is our sin. We truly believed what those secular politicians told us when they said that they want to grant us equal rights. We thought they were serious about it and not that they were saying so only to establish a coalition government. We were mistaken when we thought that others recognize our right to exist, and that perhaps at last the Zionist country, which has been innately hostile to us ever since it was founded, has changed.[19]

As this passage illustrates, orthodox Judaism remains, in some of its manifestations, non-Zionist or even anti-Zionist.

Radical Islam, like orthodox Judaism, speaks with many voices. In neither case is there any universally recognized fount of authoritative doctrine, like the Pope. Among Israeli Arabs (or, as many now prefer to style themselves, Palestinian citizens of Israel), a strong Islamic movement has emerged in recent years. It is divided between moderate and militant factions: the former, led by the movement's founder, Sheikh Abdallah Darwish, favours integration within Israeli politics and society; the latter, headed by Sheikh Ra'id Salah, mayor of Umm al-Fahm, is close to the Hamas movement based in Gaza.[20] Darwish called suicide bombers 'criminals', while the opposing faction expressed 'understanding' for their motives.[21]

One way of understanding such phenomena is to acknowledge the empirical reality that religion, a human cultural construct, is being constantly reformulated. In both Jewish and Islamic traditions some elements tend towards quietism and others towards militancy. Responding to varying internal and external impulses, one or other of these competing tendencies may, at different periods, rise to the surface. Neither can claim exclusive historical authenticity. The notion that Judaism and Islam are 'inherently' antagonistic or 'essentially' unable to live with each other cannot stand up to serious historical examination.[22]

Nor should the religious sanction claimed by some terrorists be regarded as a predominant form of legitimation within either Zionism or Palestinian nationalism. Both of these are primarily secular movements. Religious Zionism was always a minority within the Zionist movement, just as Zionists were a minority within orthodox Judaism. Palestinian nationalism, it is true, had a strong Islamic flavour in the mandatory period under the leadership of Hajj Amin al-Husayni. But while Islam is undeniably a major political force in the Arab world today, the Palestine Liberation Organization, since its foundation in the 1960s, has had a mainly secular character and Islamic elements have been secondary and subordinate.

Secular nationalism may, of course, be as dogmatic, uncompromising, and violent as political doctrines claiming religious sanction. Both Zionism and Palestinian nationalism contain significant strands that resist any form of accommodation and aim at the total destruction of the other. For the Israeli far right the idea of 'transfer' retains an illusive allure. In 2002, a large minority of the Israeli Jewish public, reacting to the growth of terrorist attacks, embraced this supposed solution to the security and demographic challenges that they faced. Slogans calling for the expulsion of Palestinians and even of Arab citizens of Israel migrated from wall graffiti to bumper stickers, mainstream political discourse and television talk shows. At the same time support ballooned among Palestinians for those (not only Islamists) who call for the elimination of the State of Israel and the expulsion of all Jews who arrived there after 1917.

But within both Israel and Palestine since the outbreak of the second intifada a vigorous internal debate has raged over means as well as ends. Both national movements have shown, in the course of their history, a capacity to evolve in order to meet changing strategic, diplomatic, and demographic conditions. A critical point for Zionism came in 1937 when, after bitter internal debate, it accepted the principle of partition. For the Palestinian movement a similar moment of truth came in the decade after 1982 when, following prolonged and acrimonious argument, the decision was taken to accept the existence of Israel and to embark on the path of negotiation. The notion that either Zionism or Palestinian nationalism is 'essentially' or 'inherently' devoted to the elimination of the other fails to take into account the internal divisions within each of them and the demonstrated capacity of both to change.

All ideologies evolve to reflect changing social realities – or they wither and die. Zionism, no doubt because it gives expression to the aspirations of a more dynamic society, has adapted much more effectively than Palestinian nationalism. The political scientist Yaron Ezrahi has charted the growing strength of individualistic as distinct from collective values in Israel in recent years.[23] And the country's conception of nationhood itself is being transformed in a process that the sociologist Baruch Kimmerling identifies as a 'decline of Israeliness'.[24] The trend has accelerated as a result of the privatization and diversification of the Israeli economy, the increasingly cosmopolitan make-up of the Israeli population, and the growing influence of American culture and pluralistic value-systems.

Palestinian society and its attendant values are also in flux. And Israel itself is a significant motor for such change. The proposition is often advanced, especially by Israeli doves, that (as a writer in *Ha'aretz* put it in August 2002): 'Occupation corrupts the basic norms of the occupier. It forces the occupier to deviate from its standard practices. It creates discrimination and inequality. By definition, it violates the rights of the individual.'[25] No doubt at a theoretical level and in a world in which there was no hypocrisy, self-deception, or conflicting values, this would be true – as well as being an excellent debating point. But in the real world we have many examples that tend in a sadly different direction. The British

Empire is one such case: the growth of liberalism and humane values at home managed to co-exist for a long time with repression and denial of those same rights in colonial possessions. One might indeed argue much more persuasively for an opposite cause–effect relationship – an 'export' rather than an 'import' model: liberalism at home, rather than being contaminated by colonial repression abroad, is often exported to colonies, internalized by the intelligentsia of the colonized nation, and then deployed as a weapon against the colonizer. Again the history of the final phase of the British Empire offers several such examples.

In the case of Israel and Palestine, there is some evidence that the 'export' model is no less applicable than the 'import' model. Palestinian society, more perhaps than most others in the Arab world, has opened itself up in recent decades to what may loosely be termed 'civil society' values. Since 1967 it has become much more complex, variegated, sophisticated – a product of urbanization, growth in literacy and secondary and tertiary education, the influence of mass media, as well as of the example of Israel. The late 1990s saw the emergence in Palestine of green shoots of pluralism, autonomous institutions led, in many cases, by independent-minded, often Western-educated, people. As in the case of anti-colonial movements in the British and French empires, concepts have been embraced and copied from the colonial power, partly to be turned as weapons against the enemy, partly out of a half-conscious, seldom-stated admiration for the success of the colonizing society and a desire to emulate its achievements.

Critics of the Palestinian Authority justly point out that the internalization of liberal values has been, to say the least, incomplete. The concepts of the rule of law and judicial independence got off to a rocky start in the Palestinian territories. Human rights were often subordinated to political and security needs: arbitrary arrests, abuse of administrative authority, interference with the courts, and suppression of freedom of the media were widespread. Israel frequently pressed the Palestinian Authority for harsh action against extremist dissidents – and then criticized it for resorting to undemocratic methods. The outbreak of the second intifada was followed by some shocking and highly publicized incidents of mob violence directed against prisoners, both Israeli and Palestinian, in police custody or even during court proceedings. On the other hand, pressure, internal as well as external, for reform of Palestinian institutions led in September 2002 to the rejection by the Palestinian Council of Yasir Arafat's reconstituted Cabinet, a significant assertion of authority by the legislature at the expense of the executive. The struggle for the soul of Palestine, as of Israel, remains unresolved.

Since the start of the second intifada, and under the impact of Palestinian terrorism and Israeli counter-attacks, opinion among both Israelis and Palestinians has radicalized. But at the same time a contradictory picture emerges: both peoples evince a greater tolerance of violence as a means of achieving political ends; yet both sustain majorities that are prepared to accept a 'two-state' solution.

An opinion poll in the West Bank and Gaza, conducted in

August 2002, showed that for the first time support for militant Islamist groups had overtaken that for Arafat's secular-nationalist Fateh organization (27 per cent to 26 per cent respectively). Although Arafat remained the most popular political figure, support for him had declined to 34 per cent from 46 per cent in July 2000, before the outbreak of the second intifada. As many as 85 per cent believed that corruption existed in PA institutions and 84 per cent supported fundamental reforms in the Palestinian Authority. A majority, 52 per cent, supported the continued bombing attacks against civilians inside Israel, though opinion was more or less evenly divided between those supporting and those opposing a cease-fire in return for Israeli withdrawal. Seventy per cent believed that armed struggle would be more effective than negotiation in securing Palestinian national rights. But an even higher percentage, 73 per cent, supported reconciliation between the two peoples based on a peace agreement and a two-state solution.[26]

A similar dissonance could be observed in Israeli Jewish opinion. Polls between 1987 and 1997 showed steady growth in acceptance of the concept of a Palestinian state. Before the Oslo agreements, only a small minority favoured this; but by 1997 51 per cent did so – on condition that it resulted in peace. The failure of the Camp David summit and the outbreak of the second intifada increased the proportions of those favouring such measures as the arrest and deportation of Arafat, destruction of the Palestinian Authority, and mass expulsion of Arabs from both the occupied territories and Israel itself. Yet side by side with such views, and seemingly without a sense of internal contradiction, a majority of Israelis continued to believe that a Palestinian state would probably come into being and that it was a necessary feature of any long-term peace agreement. A poll of settlers in July 2002 indicated a surprising readiness on the part of a majority of them to leave their homes in return for compensation: 68 per cent said they would comply with any such decision by the country's democratic institutions while only 2 per cent said they would resist by force.[27] Another poll in October 2002 showed no fewer than 78 per cent of Israeli Jews favouring withdrawal from most of the settlements.[28]

The struggle between competing social aspirations and sets of cultural values within both Israel and Palestine will not be decided by majority votes. Terrorists do not need a majority. Liberals have learned to their cost in many political conflicts that a mere majority is not enough. Nor is it to be expected that swords will be broken into ploughshares as the result of a sudden outbreak on all sides of reasonableness and amity. Wish fulfilment is not a method of conflict resolution. 'We win the wars we did not fight and the peace that was never signed ushers in a golden age,' warned an earlier historian of Israeli–Arab relations.[29] Nevertheless, peace, if it is to come at all, will be attained only as a result of transformations in collective human consciousness. The most compelling sources of such change are likely to be the demographic, socio-economic, environmental, and territorial imperatives that have been examined in this book and that press down ever more strenuously on the two protagonists. If any form of civilized human existence is to survive in their common homeland, these ineluctable forces must eventually bring Israelis and Palestinians to terms.

Chronology

1831–9

    Egyptian occupation of Palestine

1881

    Assassination of Tsar Alexander II spurs pogroms: large-scale Jewish emigration from Russian Empire begins

1882

    Start of modern Jewish settlement in Palestine ('first *aliya*')

1896

    Publication of Theodor Herzl's *The Jewish State*

1897

    First Zionist Congress in Basel

1902

    Joseph Chamberlain proposes Jewish settlement in British East Africa

1903

Kishinev pogrom; start of 'second *aliya*', wave of socialist-Zionist immigration

1904

Death of Herzl

1905

Seventh Zionist Congress rejects East Africa project

1908

Young Turk revolution re-establishes Ottoman parliament

1913

First Arab Nationalist Congress in Paris

1915

Anglo-Arab McMahon–Husayn correspondence promises Arab state in return for revolt against Turks

1916

Anglo-French Sykes–Picot pact agrees post-war disposition of Fertile Crescent

1917

2 November   British government issues Balfour

Declaration in support of Zionism

9 December   British conquest of Jerusalem

1918

31 October   Mudros Armistice: Turkey withdraws from war; Britain controls Palestine

1919

3 January   Faisal–Weizmann agreement signed in Paris

1920

April   Anti-Zionist riots in Jerusalem

San Remo Conference allots Palestine mandate to Britain

1 July   Sir Herbert Samuel takes office as High Commissioner in Palestine

December   Palestine Arab Congress meets in Haifa

1921

1 May   Anti-Zionist riots in Jaffa

8 May   Hajj Amin al-Husayni appointed Grand Mufti of Jerusalem

May   Palestine Arab Congress meets in Jerusalem

July   Palestine Arab Delegation visits London

December   Supreme Muslim Council created

1922

March   Mufti elected President of Supreme Muslim Council

3 June	Churchill White Paper issued, promising Legislative Council
24 July	League of Nations Council approves mandate for Palestine
23 October	First Palestine census

1923

Arabs boycott elections; Legislative Council plan dropped

1929

August   Anti-Jewish riots in Jerusalem, Hebron and elsewhere

1930

20 October   Report by Sir John Hope-Simpson published

1931

14 February   British government reaffirms pro-Zionist policy

18 November   Second Palestine census

16 December   World Islamic Conference meets in Jerusalem

1933

30 January   Hitler takes office as German Chancellor

October   Arab nationalist riots

1935

October   Arab guerrilla group led by Sheikh Izz ed-Din al-Qassam destroyed by British forces

1936

15 April   Start of Arab general revolt
25 April   Arab Higher Committee, headed by Mufti, formed

1937

7 July   Royal Commission report proposes partition

1939

February–March   St James's Palace Conference fails to reach agreement
17 May   Palestine White Paper restricts Jewish immigration to 75,000 over five years

1939–45

Mass murder of six million Jews in Europe

1945

22 March   Arab League Pact signed in Cairo

1946

1 May   Anglo-American committee proposes admission of 100,000 Jewish refugees to Palestine

| 22 July | King David Hotel blown up by Jewish terrorists: ninety dead |

1947

| 18 February | Britain announces intention to hand back mandate to United Nations |
| 29 November | UN General Assembly votes for partition of Palestine into Jewish and Arab states |

1948

14 May	End of British mandate; State of Israel declared
	Israel wins decisive military victories over invading Arab states
	700,000 Palestinian Arabs displaced from their homes
	Large-scale Jewish immigration from Europe and Arab lands begins
December	Transjordan annexes West Bank: Abdullah declared King of Jordan

1949

| February–July | Israel signs armistice agreements with Egypt, Jordan, Lebanon, and Syria |

1951

| 20 July | Assassination of King Abdullah |

1952

23 July | Officers' coup overthrows monarchy in Egypt
7 December | Moshe Sharett succeeds David Ben-Gurion as Israeli Prime Minister

1955

2 November | Ben-Gurion returns as Israeli Prime Minister

1956

26 July | President Nasser nationalizes Suez Canal
24 October | Secret agreement at Sèvres by Britain, France, and Israel to attack Egypt
29 October | Israel invades Sinai
5 November | Britain and France launch abortive attack on Egypt

1957

January | Israel withdraws from Sinai
March | Israel withdraws from Gaza Strip
October | France signs secret agreement to transfer nuclear materials and know-how to Israel

1958

1 February | Egypt and Syria form United Arab Republic
14 July | Military coup overthrows monarchy in Iraq
Fateh movement founded in Kuwait

1964

29 May   Palestine Liberation Organization founded
                under Arab League auspices

1967

May   Nasser orders UN forces out of Sinai and
                blockades Straits of Tiran

5–11 June   Israel scores decisive victory over Egypt,
                Syria, and Jordan in Six-Day War; occupies
                Sinai, Gaza Strip, West Bank, and Golan
                Heights

22 November   UN Security Council passes Resolution 242
                calling for Israeli withdrawal to secure and
                recognized boundaries

1969

March   Start of Egypt/Israel war of attrition along
                Suez Canal
                Golda Meir becomes Prime Minister of
                Israel

1970

August   Israel and Egypt agree to truce, ending war
                of attrition

September   Anwar Sadat becomes President of Egypt
                after death of Nasser
                'Black September': Jordan drives out PLO

1972

30 May	Terrorist attack on Tel Aviv airport
September	Terrorist attack on Israeli athletes at Munich Olympics

1973

6 October	Start of Yom Kippur War (War of Ramadan)
21 October	UN Security Council Resolution 338 calls for cease-fire and direct talks
11 November	Egypt–Israel cease-fire agreement signed
21 December	Middle East peace conference opens in Geneva but adjourns after one day

1974

18 January	Israel and Egypt sign separation-of-forces agreement
10 April	Resignation of Golda Meir as Israeli Prime Minister, to be succeeded by Yitzhak Rabin
5 June	Israel and Syria sign disengagement agreement on Golan Heights
26–29 October	Arab League conference in Rabat recognizes PLO as sole representative of Palestinians
13 November	Yasir Arafat addresses UN General Assembly

1975

13 April	Outbreak of Lebanese civil war
5 June	Suez Canal, closed since 1967, reopens
1 September	Israel and Egypt sign 'Sinai II' disengagement agreement

10 November   UN General Assembly pronounces Zionism
'a form of racism'

1977

17 May   Menahem Begin wins election victory to
head first non-Labour government in Israel

19–21   President Anwar Sadat of Egypt visits
November   Jerusalem

1978

17 September Israel and Egypt sign Camp David
agreement

1979

26 March   Israel–Egypt peace treaty

1981

7 June   Israel destroys Iraqi Osirak nuclear facility
6 October   Sadat assassinated; Hosni Mubarak succeeds
him as President of Egypt

1982

26 April   Israel completes withdrawal from Sinai
(except Taba)
6 June   Israeli invasion of Lebanon
16 September Falangist massacre of Palestinians in Sabra
and Shatila refugee camps near Beirut

1983

February
Judicial commission finds Ariel Sharon 'remiss in his duties' and forces his resignation from Israeli Defence Ministry

17 May
Abortive Israeli–Lebanese peace treaty signed

28 August
Begin resigns as Israeli Prime Minister to be succeeded by Yitzhak Shamir

1984

14 September
Shimon Peres heads Israeli National Unity government

1986

20 October
Shamir replaces Peres as Israeli Prime Minister

1987

8 December
First intifada begins

1988

31 July
King Hussein of Jordan cuts links with West Bank

December
Addressing UN, Arafat renounces terrorism

After arbitration, Israel withdraws from Taba

USSR opens door to free Jewish emigration

1990

2 August
Iraq invades Kuwait

1991

| 16 January | US bombing of Iraq marks start of Gulf War |
| 30 October | Middle East peace conference opens in Madrid |

1992

| 23 June | Yitzhak Rabin elected Prime Minister of Israel |

1993

| 13 September | Rabin and Arafat sign first 'Oslo Agreement' in Washington |

1994

25 February	Baruch Goldstein kills twenty-nine Arabs at Tomb of Patriarchs in Hebron
May	Israel withdraws from Jericho and part of Gaza Strip
July	Arafat returns to Palestine to head Palestinian Authority
26 October	Israel–Jordan peace treaty

1995

| 28 September | 'Oslo II' Agreement on further Israeli withdrawal in West Bank |
| 4 November | Assassination of Yitzhak Rabin |

1996

| 21 January | First Palestinian elections |

February	Fifty-eight killed in terror bombings in Jerusalem and Tel Aviv
11 April	Israeli attack on Lebanon: 100 Palestinians killed in UN compound at Qana
29 May	Binyamin Netanyahu defeats Shimon Peres in Israeli elections

1997

15 January	Israeli–Palestinian agreement on Hebron

1998

23 October	Netanyahu and Arafat sign Wye River Memorandum on further Israeli withdrawal from parts of West Bank (not implemented)

1999

7 February	Death of King Hussein of Jordan; succeeded by Abdullah II
17 May	Ehud Barak defeats Netanyahu in Israeli election

2000

24 May	Israel completes withdrawal from southern Lebanon
10 June	Death of President Hafiz al-Assad of Syria; succeeded by son Bashar
July	Arafat and Barak fail to agree at Camp David summit
28 September	Sharon visits Temple Mount Start of second intifada

2001

January	Israeli–Palestinian talks at Taba suspended after coming closer to agreement
6 February	Sharon defeats Barak in Israeli election
11 September	Arab terrorist attacks on New York and Washington

2002

March	Palestinian terror attacks kill 127 Israelis
28 March	Arab League approves Saudi peace proposals Israel reoccupies much of West Bank
24 June	President Bush calls for 'provisional' Palestinian state under new leadership
November	Israel Labour Party withdraws from National Unity government and elects Amram Mitzna its leader

2003

28 January	Israeli elections

Notes

Chapter 1 **People**

1 See, for example, David Landes, 'Palestine before the Zionists', *Commentary*, 61: 2 (Feb. 1976), pp. 47–56, and Fred Gottheil, 'The Population of Palestine, Circa 1875', *Middle Eastern Studies*, 15: 3 (Oct. 1979), pp. 310–21.

2 Joan Peters, *From Time Immemorial: The Origins of the Arab–Jewish Conflict over Palestine* (New York, 1984).

3 See the critique by Yehoshua Porath in *New York Review of Books*, 16 January 1986, and subsequent debate in issue dated 27 March 1986; also Justin McCarthy, *The Population of Palestine: Population History and Statistics of the Late Ottoman Period and the Mandate* (New York, 1990), esp. pp. 40–1.

4 McCarthy, *Population of Palestine*, pp. 13–27.

5 See his review of McCarthy in *Middle Eastern Studies*, 28: 4 (Oct. 1992), pp. 803–7.

6 *Ha'aretz*, 17 July 2001.

7 Leonard Stein, *The Balfour Declaration* (London, 1961).

8 Bernard Wasserstein, *The British in Palestine: The Mandatory Government and the Arab–Jewish Conflict, 1917–1929* (2nd edn, Oxford, 1991), p. 88.

9 M. Mossek, *Palestine Immigration Policy under Sir Herbert*

Samuel: British, Zionist and Arab Attitudes (London, 1978).

10 Samuel to Weizmann, 29 Nov. 1920, Central Zionist Archives [henceforward CZA] Z4/15445; see also Bernard Wasserstein, *Herbert Samuel: A Political Life* (Oxford, 1992), p. 254.

11 Memorandum by Arlosoroff, 15 April 1929, CZA, Jerusalem, Gimel 25.448.

12 Memorandum (in German) by Ruppin, 15 March 1929, ibid.

13 Eric Mills, *Census of Palestine 1931*, vol. I, Report (Alexandria, 1933), pp. 45 and 329–40.

14 On the Indian basis, see Sir John Chancellor to Sir John Shuckburgh, 3 July 1931, Public Record Office [henceforth PRO] CO 733/206/5A, and Colonial Office minute [signature illegible], 15 June 1931, ibid.

15 Undated memorandum by Mills, ibid.

16 Chancellor to Sir John Shuckburgh, 10 July 1931, ibid.

17 Minutes of meeting of Arab Census Advisory Committee, 24 June 1931, ibid.

18 Mills, *Census 1931*, vol. I, p. 73.

19 Minutes of meeting of Jewish Census Advisory Committee, 6 July 1931, PRO CO 733/206/5A, and Chancellor to Shuckburgh, 8 Aug. 1931, ibid. Also minutes by Shuckburgh et al., June 1931, ibid.

20 Translated extract from Hebrew pamphlet entitled 'The *Yishuv* and the Census', 22 Oct. 1931, in PRO CO 733/206/5B.

21 *Statistical Abstract of Palestine, 1939* (Jerusalem, 1939), pp. ii–iii.

22 E. Mills, 'The Fertility of Marriage in Palestine', special bulletin 3 (1939), Office of Statistics, Jerusalem, copy in PRO CO 733/415/1.

23 Rita Hinden, 'The Fertility and Mortality of the Population of Palestine', *Sociological Review*, 33 (1940), pp. 29–49. See also *Statistical Abstract of Palestine 1943* (Jerusalem, 1943), pp. 6–7.

24 W. D. Battershill (Jerusalem) to H. F. Downie (Colonial Office), 12 Jan. 1939, enclosing memoranda by Mills, PRO CO 733/387/7.

25 Minute by J. S. Bennett, 10 Jan. 1939, PRO CO 733/387/7. On the results of the White Paper policy, see Bernard Wasserstein, *Britain and the Jews of Europe, 1939-1945* (London, 1979).

26 Gabriel Sheffer, *Moshe Sharett: Biography of a Political Moderate* (Oxford, 1996), p. 734.

27 *New York Times*, 19 Oct. 1987.

28 For a fuller discussion of the background to this point, see Bernard Wasserstein, *Vanishing Diaspora* (London, revised edn, 1997).

29 *New York Times*, 20 Aug. 1981.

30 *Jerusalem Post*, 17 July 2001, and *Guardian*, 23 July 2001.

31 *al-Ahram* (weekly online edition), 11–17 Oct. 2001.

32 *Ha'aretz*, 19 March 2002.

33 *Jerusalem Report*, 5 Nov. 2001.

Chapter 2 **Society**

1 Quoted in Zachary Lockman, *Comrades and Enemies: Arab and Jewish Workers in Palestine 1906–1948* (Berkeley, 1996), pp. 41–2.

2 Oz Almog, *The Sabra: The Creation of the New Jew* (Berkeley, 2000), p. 2.

3 Quoted ibid., p. 157.

4 Baruch Nadel, quoted ibid., p. 280.

5 Isaac Deutscher, *The Non-Jewish Jew and Other Essays* (London, 1968).

6 Quoted in Almog, *Sabra*, p. 87.

7 Ibid., p. 106.

8 Ibid., pp. 27–9.

9 Gershon Shaked, 'Shall We Find Sufficient Strength? On Behalf of Israeli Secularism', *Israel Affairs*, 4: 3 & 4 (Spring/Summer 1998), pp. 82, 85.

10 See Derek Penslar, *Zionism and Technocracy: The Engineering of Jewish Settlement in Palestine, 1870–1918* (Bloomington, 1991), p. 19.

11 The definition of 'rurality' has changed over the period. Larger communities than in earlier times are now considered 'rural'.

12 The figures (from the Israel Central Bureau of Statistics) are not strictly comparable, as there was a reclassification of categories in 1995, but the general trend holds. These figures include both Jews and non-Jews. They apply only to Israel, not to the West Bank and Gaza.

13 See tables in Jacob Metzer, *The Divided Economy of Mandatory Palestine* (Cambridge, 1998), pp. 240–1.

1

14 See ibid., p. 198.
15 Meir Yaish, 'Class Structure in a Deeply Divided Society: Class and Ethnic Equality in Israel, 1974–1991', *British Journal of Sociology*, 52: 3 (Sept. 2001), pp. 409–39.
16 Barbara S. Okun, 'The Effects of Ethnicity and Educational Attainment on Jewish Marriage Patterns: Changes in Israel 1957–1995', *Population Studies*, 55 (2001), pp. 49–64.
17 Gershon Shafir and Yoav Peled, *Being Israeli: The Dynamics of Multiple Citizenship* (Cambridge, 2002), pp. 82–4.
18 Yaakov Kop and Robert E. Litan, *Sticking Together: The Israeli Experiment in Pluralism* (Washington, D.C., 2002), pp. 103–5.
19 *Ha'aretz*, 3 Dec. 2002.
20 Ira Sharkansky, 'A Critical Look at Israel's Economic and Social Gaps' (unpublished draft paper, 2002).
21 See, for example, Robert Lerman, 'US Income Equality Trends and Recent Immigration', paper presented to the Population Association of America, 23 March 2000.
22 Shafir and Peled, *Being Israeli*, p. 43.
23 Avraham Pavin, *The Kibbutz Movement: Facts and Figures 2001* (Yad Tabenkin, Ramat Efal, 2001 (in Hebrew)).
24 *Ha'aretz*, 7 Nov. 2002.
25 Uriel Levitan, 'Faith on the Decline', *Kibbutz Trends*, 29: 1 (Spring 1998), pp. 57–8.
26 Joshua Muravchik, 'Socialism's Last Stand', *Commentary*, 113: 3 (March 2002), pp. 47–53.

27 Daniel Gavron, *The Kibbutz: Awakening from Utopia* (Lanham, Md., 2000), p. 1.

28 Kenneth W. Stein, 'Palestine's Rural Economy, 1917–1939', *Studies in Zionism*, 8: 1 (1987), pp. 25–49.

29 Kenneth W. Stein, *The Land Question in Palestine, 1917–1939* (Chapel Hill, 1984).

30 *Palestine: Report on Immigration, Land Settlement and Development*, Cmd 3686 (London, 1930).

31 The dunam, a Turkish measure of area, is still used in Israel/Palestine. 1 metric dunam = 0.25 acres or approximately 1,000m^2.

32 See Roza I. M. El-Eini, 'The Implementation of British Agricultural Policy in Palestine in the 1930s', *Middle Eastern Studies*, 32: 4 (Oct. 1996), pp. 211–50.

33 *Report of a Committee on the Economic Condition of Agriculturists in Palestine and the Fiscal Measures of Government in Relation Thereto* (Jerusalem, 1930), *passim*.

34 Lewis French, *Supplementary Report on Agricultural Development and Land Settlement in Palestine* (Jerusalem, 1932), p. 59.

35 Stein, *Land Question*, p. 146.

36 Lewis French, *First Report on Agricultural Development and Land Settlement in Palestine* (Jerusalem, 1931), p. 5.

37 French, *Supplementary Report*, p. 60.

38 Ibid., p. 19.

39 Metzer, *Divided Economy*, p. 93.

40 *Report of a Committee on the Economic Condition of Agriculturists*, pp. 41–2.

41 Ibid., p. 48.

42 Mills, *Census 1931*, vol. I, p. 51.

43 See Metzer, *Divided Economy*, pp. 148–9.

44 Amira Hass, *Drinking the Sea at Gaza: Days and Nights in a Land under Siege* (New York, 1999), p. 177.

45 World Bank Report No. 22312-GZ, *Poverty in the West Bank and Gaza* (World Bank, 18 June 2001).

46 *Ha'aretz*, 23 Aug. 2002.

47 World Bank, *Fifteen Months – Intifada, Closures and Palestinian Economic Crisis: An Assessment* (World Bank, 18 March 2002), p. v.

48 World Bank, *Fifteen Months*, p. 35.

49 See Avram S. Bornstein, *Crossing the Green Line: Between the West Bank and Israel* (Philadelphia, 2002), pp. 44 and 142.

50 State of Israel Ministry of Labour and Social Affairs, Oct. 1983.

51 World Bank, *Fifteen Months*, p. 14.

52 Zeev Schiff and Ehud Ya'ari, *Intifada: The Palestinian Uprising – Israel's Third Front* (New York, 1990), p. 149.

53 This account is based on World Bank data but Bornstein, *Crossing the Line*, pp. 51 and 143, gives a different chronology of the rise and fall of Arab labour in Israel.

54 World Bank, *Fifteen Months*, p. 13.

55 World Bank, *Poverty in the West Bank and Gaza*, p. 63.

56 World Bank, *Fifteen Months*, p. v.

57 *Ha'aretz*, 23 Aug. 2002. Figures from Palestine Central Bureau of Statistics. The PCBS used a broad definition

of unemployment, similar to that favoured by the International Labor Organization, which includes in the labour force so-called 'discouraged workers' who are not actively seeking work. The narrowly defined labour force declined from 735,000 in the third quarter of 2000 to 680,000 in the second quarter of 2002.

58 *Jerusalem Post*, 5 Nov. 2002.
59 *Jerusalem Post*, 6 March 2002.
60 Figures from Israel Central Bureau of Statistics.
61 *Ha'aretz*, 6 March 2002.
62 *Jerusalem Post*, 5 Nov. 2002.
63 *Ha'aretz*, 22 Nov. 1999; *Jerusalem Post*, 11 Jan. 2001.
64 *International Herald Tribune*, 3 July 1998.
65 *Jerusalem Post*, 28 Oct. 1999.

Chapter 3 **Environment**

1 Figures from Israel Central Bureau of Statistics and Palestine Central Bureau of Statistics.
2 Penslar, *Zionism and Technocracy*, pp. 74–5.
3 *Encyclopaedia Judaica* (Jerusalem, 1970), vol. ix, col. 788.
4 Nurit Kliot, 'Forests and Forest Fires in Israel', *International Forest Fire News*, 15 (Sept. 1996). Definitions of forest cover vary. According to another definition, Israel's forest cover is 4.95 per cent. By most criteria, however, Israel is among countries regarded as having low forest cover. The UN Food and Agriculture Organization regards countries having less than 0.07

hectares of forest per person as below the minimum
required level. Israel has 0.021 hectares of forest per
person. Another measure is the ratio of current to
'original' forest area (based upon ecological maps
depicting 'what areas may have been forested 8000 years
ago'): in Israel's case only 4.2 per cent of the supposedly
'original' forested area remains. See H. Gyde Lund et
al., 'Definition of Low Forest Cover (LFC)', United
Nations Environment Program and International Union
of Forest Research Organizations, 2000.

5 Taufik Canaan, *Mohammedan Saints and Sanctuaries in
   Palestine* (London, 1927), p. 34.

6 Ibid, p. 71.

7 See Meron Benvenisti, *Sacred Landscape: The Buried
   History of the Holy Land since 1948* (Berkeley, 2000), pp.
   251–6.

8 Applied Research Institute – Jerusalem, *The Status of the
   Environment in the West Bank* (Bethlehem, 1997), pp.
   138–9.

9 R. F. Jardine to District Commissioner, Haifa, 17 Jan.
   1944, Israel State Archives (henceforth ISA)
   2/480/V/12/44.

10 Water Commissioner to Chief Secretary, 16 Feb. 1946,
   ibid.

11 NBC News, 10 Oct. 1999.

12 Walter C. Lowdermilk, *Palestine: Land of Promise* (New
   York, 1944).

13 George Adam Smith, *The Historical Geography of the Holy
   Land* (2nd edn, London, 1894), pp. 472 and 481.

14 Tamar Zohary and K. David Hambright, 'Lake Hula –
    Lake Agmon: Human Development and Nature in the
    Hula Valley', *Israel Review of Arts and Letters*, 109 (1999),
    pp. 71–87.

15 *Jerusalem Post*, 24 March 2002.

16 Mills, *Census 1931,* vol. I, p. 13.

17 Robert R. Nathan, Oscar Gass, and Daniel Creamer,
    Palestine: Problem and Promise (Washington, DC, 1946),
    p. 163.

18 J. A. Allan, 'Middle Eastern Hydropolitics: Interpreting
    Constructed Knowledge', *Geopolitics* 3: 2 (Autumn
    1998), pp. 125–32.

19 Wayne B. Solley, Robert R. Pierce and Howard R.
    Perlman, *Estimated Use of Water in the United States in
    1995* (Washington, DC, 1998); cf. *New York Times*, 28
    Aug. 2002.

20 J. A. Allan, *The Middle East Water Question: Hydropolitics
    and the Global Economy* (London, 2002), pp. 5–6.

21 Ibid., p. 79.

22 Ibid., pp. 39–40.

23 'Israel's Water Economy', Israel Foreign Ministry,
    August 2002.

24 Figures from Israel Ministry of National Infrastructures.

25 Greg Shapland, *Rivers of Discord: International Water
    Disputes in the Middle East* (New York, 1997), p. 20.

26 Ibid., p. 22.

27 Schiff and Ya'ari, *Intifada*, p. 97.

28 Report on Israel Channel 2 TV, 1700 GMT, 9 July 2002
    (BBC Monitoring Report).

29 *Ha'aretz*, 22 Oct. 2002.

30 *The Times*, 4 July 2000.

31 Marwan Haddad, Eran Feitelson, Shaul Arlosoroff, and Taher Nasseredin, *Joint Management of Shared Aquifers: An Implementation-Oriented Agenda: Final Report of Phase II* (Jerusalem, 1999), p. 1.

32 Ibid., p. ix.

33 Israel Foreign Ministry. See also *Ha'aretz*, 13 Feb. 2001.

34 Israel Foreign Ministry, 'Sustainable Development in the Palestinian Authority' (Jerusalem, August 2002).

35 Haddad et al., *Final Report*, p. 47.

Chapter 4 **Territory**

1 See, for example, Louis René Beres, 'After the "Peace Process": Israel, Palestine and Regional Nuclear War', *Dickinson Journal of International Law*, 15: 2 (Winter 1997), pp. 301–35. The author is a political scientist at Purdue University in Indiana who is close to the Israeli Likud Party.

2 See, for example, Ziad Abu-Zayyad, 'Land: The Core of the Conflict', *Palestine-Israel Journal*, 4: 2 (1999). The author served for several years in the Palestinian Authority as Minister for Jerusalem Affairs.

3 Akram Hanieh, 'The Camp David Papers', *Journal of Palestine Studies*, 30: 2 (Winter 2001), pp. 75–97.

4 Samuel to Sir W. Tyrrell, 5 June 1919, *Documents on British Foreign Policy 1919–1939*, First Series, vol. IV (London, 1952), pp. 283–5.

5 Memorandum by Balfour for Lloyd George, 26 June 1919, pp. 301–3.

6 Curzon to Lord Hardinge, 26 April 1920, *Documents on British Foreign Policy 1919–1939*, First Series, vol. XIII (London, 1963), pp. 251–2.

7 *Palestine Royal Commission Report* (Cmd 5479, London, 1937), p. 391.

8 Benny Morris, *Righteous Victims: A History of the Zionist–Arab Conflict, 1881–1999* (New York, 1999), pp. 139–44.

9 'Observations on the Partition Proposals' by Leonard Stein, 4 Aug. 1937, Leonard Stein Papers, Bodleian Library, Oxford, Box 112.

10 Memorandum by Eric Mills, 2 Dec. 1937, forwarded to Colonial Office by the High Commissioner, Sir Arthur Wauchope, 14 Dec. 1937, PRO CO 733/354/4.

11 *Palestine Gazette* announcement quoted in Moshe Shertok (Jewish Agency) to Chief Secretary, Government of Palestine, 3 July 1939, ISA 2/551/Y/ 55/39.

12 Ibid.

13 B. G. Bourdillon (Acting Chief Secretary) to Director of Broadcasting, 21 Sept. 1945, ibid.

14 Shertok to Chief Secretary, 3 July 1939, ibid.

15 R. [Couch?] (Nablus) to Chief Secretary, 30 Jan. 1941, ibid.

16 See Bernard Wasserstein, *Divided Jerusalem: The Struggle for the Holy City* (rev. edn, London, 2002), pp. 208–16.

17 David Newman, 'Creating the Fences of Territorial

Separation: The Discourses of Israeli–Palestinian
Conflict Resolution', *Geopolitics and International
Boundaries*, 2: 2 (Autumn 1997), p. 5.
18 *Ha'aretz*, 15 March 2002.
19 Most of these figures are drawn from a report issued in
draft form in May 2002 by B'Tselem Israeli
Information Center for Human Rights in the Occupied
Territories and entitled 'Land Grab: Israel's Settlement
Policy in the West Bank'.
20 Ibid.

Chapter 5 **Dynamics of political change**

1 *Ha'aretz*, 23 Aug. 2002.
2 *New York Times*, 25 Nov. 2002.
3 *Ha'aretz*, 27 Nov. 2002.
4 Hussein Agha and Robert Malley, 'The Tragedy of
Errors', *New York Review of Books*, 9 Aug. 2001; Ari Shavit,
interview with former Israeli Foreign Minister Shlomo
Ben-Ami, *Ha'aretz*, 13 Sept. 2001; *New York Times*, 26
July 2001; Akram Hanieh, 'The Camp David Papers',
Journal of Palestine Studies, 30: 2 (Winter 2001), pp.
75–97.
5 *Ha'aretz*, 15 Feb. 2002.
6 *New York Review of Books*, 13 June 2002.
7 *Ha'aretz*, 22 Feb. 2002.
8 http://info.jpost.com/1999/Supplements/Elections99/
candidates/barak3.shtml.
9 *New York Times*, 15 Oct. 2001.

10   *Ha'aretz*, 22 April 2002.

11   *Ha'aretz*, 13 June 2002.

12   These figures are as of June 2001: *Report of the Commissioner-General of the United Nations Relief and Works Agency for Palestinian Refugees in the Near East 1 July 2000 – 30 June 2001, United Nations General Assembly Official Records, Fifty-Sixth Session, Supplement No. 13 (A/56/13)*; see also *New York Times*, 16 April 2002.

13   *New York Review of Books*, 13 June 2002; see Benny Morris, *The Birth of the Palestinian Refugee Problem, 1947–1949* (Cambridge, 1987).

14   *Middle East Peace Reports* 3: 4 (23 July 2001).

15   For a fuller discussion of the Jerusalem issue, see my *Divided Jerusalem*.

16   Ehud Sprinzak, *Brother Against Brother: Violence and Extremism in Israeli Politics from Altalena to the Rabin Assassination* (New York, 1999), pp. 259–61.

17   BBC News, 10 April 2001.

18   *Palestine Times*, 120 (June 2001).

19   Rabbi Nosson Zev Grossman, 'Thwarted Expectations', *Deiah Ve-Dibur*, 21 April 1999.

20   See Raphael Israeli, 'The Islamic Movement in Israel', *Jerusalem Center for Public Affairs Jerusalem Letter*, 416 (October 1999).

21   Nachman Tal, 'The Islamic Movement in Israel', Jaffee Center for Strategic Studies, Tel Aviv University, *Strategic Assessment*, 2: 4 (Feb. 2000).

22   See Bernard Lewis, *The Jews of Islam* (Princeton, 1984), and Norman Stillman ed., *The Jews of Arab Lands: A*

History and Source Book (Philadelphia, 1979), and idem, *The Jews of Arab Lands in Modern Times* (Philadelphia, 1991).

23 Yaron Ezrahi, *Rubber Bullets: Power and Conscience in Modern Israel* (New York, 1997).

24 Baruch Kimmerling, *The Invention and Decline of Israeliness: State, Society, and the Military* (Berkeley, 2001).

25 Amnon Rafael, 'Half-Lies, Half-Truths and Half-Justice', *Ha'aretz*, 16 Aug. 2002.

26 Press release by Palestinian Center for Policy and Survey Research, Ramallah, 26 Aug. 2002.

27 *Ha'aretz*, 25 July 2002.

28 *New York Times*, 30 Oct. 2002.

29 Christopher Sykes, *Cross Roads to Israel* (London, 1965), p. 216.

Select bibliography

Official publications

Census of Palestine 1931 (2 vols., Alexandria, 1933)
Palestine Royal Commission Report (Cmd 5479, London, 1937)
Report and General Abstracts of the Census of 1922 (Jerusalem, 1922)
Report of a Committee on the Economic Condition of Agriculturists in Palestine and the Fiscal Measures of Government in Relation Thereto (Jerusalem, 1930)
Reports on Agricultural Development and Land Settlement in Palestine by Lewis French (London/Jerusalem 1931, 1932)
Supplement to Survey of Palestine (Jerusalem, 1947)
A Survey of Palestine (3 vols., Jerusalem, 1946)

Books and articles

J. A. Allan, *The Middle East Water Question: Hydropolitics and the Global Economy* (London, 2002)
Oz Almog, *The Sabra: The Creation of the New Jew* (Berkeley, 2000)
Applied Research Institute – Jerusalem, *The Status of the Environment in the West Bank* (Bethlehem, 1997)
— *Water Resources and Irrigated Agriculture in the West Bank* (Bethlehem, 1998)

Meron Benvenisti, *Sacred Landscape: The Buried History of the Holy Land since 1948* (Berkeley, 2000)

Avram S. Bornstein, *Crossing the Green Line: Between the West Bank and Israel* (Philadelphia, 2002)

Taufik Canaan, *Mohammedan Saints and Sanctuaries in Palestine* (London, 1927)

Neil Caplan, *Palestine Jewry and the Arab Question 1917–1925* (London, 1978)

Avner Cohen, *Israel and the Bomb* (New York, 1998)

Roza I. M. El-Eini, 'The Implementation of British Agricultural Policy in Palestine in the 1930s', *Middle Eastern Studies*, 32: 4 (Oct. 1996), 211–50

Daniel Gavron, *The Kibbutz: Awakening from Utopia* (Lanham, Md., 2000)

As'ad Ghanem, *The Palestinian-Arab Minority in Israel, 1948–2000: A Political Study* (Albany, NY, 2001)

Gad G. Gilbar, *Population Dilemmas in the Middle East* (London, 1997)

Amira Hass, *Drinking the Sea at Gaza: Days and Nights in a Land under Siege* (New York, 1999)

Said B. Himadeh ed., *Economic Organization of Palestine* (Beirut, 1938)

Issa Khalaf, *Politics in Palestine: Arab Factionalism and Social Disintegration 1939–1948* (Albany, NY, 1991)

Rashid Khalidi, *Palestinian Identity: The Construction of Modern National Consciousness* (New York, 1997)

Baruch Kimmerling, *The Invention and Decline of Israeliness: State, Society, and the Military* (Berkeley, 2001)

Baruch Kimmerling and Joel S. Migdal, *Palestinians: The*

Making of a People (Cambridge, 1993)

Yaakov Kop and Robert E. Litan, *Sticking Together: The Israeli Experiment in Pluralism* (Washington, DC, 2002)

David Kretzmer, *The Occupation of Justice: The Supreme Court of Israel and the Occupied Territories* (Albany, NY, 2002)

Zachary Lockman, *Comrades and Enemies: Arab and Jewish Workers in Palestine 1906–1948* (Berkeley, 1996)

Neville Mandel, *The Arabs and Zionism before World War I* (Berkeley, 1976)

Justin McCarthy, *The Population of Palestine: Population History and Statistics of the Late Ottoman Period and the Mandate* (New York, 1990)

Jacob Metzer, *The Divided Economy of Mandatory Palestine* (Cambridge, 1998)

Benny Morris, *The Birth of the Palestinian Arab Refugee Problem, 1947–1949* (Cambridge, 1987)

— *Righteous Victims: A History of the Zionist–Arab Conflict, 1881–1999* (New York, 1999)

Moshe Mossek, *Palestine Immigration Policy under Sir Herbert Samuel: British, Zionist and Arab Attitudes* (London, 1978)

Joshua Muravchik, 'Socialism's Last Stand', *Commentary*, 113: 3 (March 2002), 47–53

David Nachmias and Gila Menahem, *Public Policy in Israel* (London, 2002)

Jodi Nachtwey and Mark Tessler, 'The Political Economy of Attitudes toward Peace among Palestinians and Israelis', *Journal of Conflict Resolution*, 46: 2 (April 2002), 260–85

Robert R. Nathan, Oscar Gass, and Daniel Creamer, *Palestine: Problem and Promise* (Washington, DC, 1946)

David Newman, 'The Territorial Politics of Exurbanization: Reflections on 25 Years of Jewish Settlement in the West Bank', *Israel Affairs*, 3: 1 (Autumn 1996), 61–85

—— 'Creating the Fences of Territorial Separation: The Discourses of Israeli–Palestinian Conflict Resolution', *Geopolitics and International Boundaries*, 2: 2 (Autumn 1997), 1–35

—— 'Population as Security: The Arab–Israeli Struggle for Demographic Hegemony', in Nana Poku and David T. Graham eds., *Redefining Security: Population Movements and National Security* (Westport, Conn., 1998), 163–85

—— 'From National to Post-national Territorial Identities in Israel-Palestine', *Geojournal*, 253 (2001), 235–46.

Barbara S. Okun, 'Religiosity and Contraceptive Method Choice: The Jewish Population of Israel', *European Journal of Population*, 16 (2000), 109–32

—— 'The Effects of Ethnicity and Educational Attainment on Jewish Marriage Patterns: Changes in Israel, 1957–1995', *Population Studies*, 55 (2001) 49–64

Roger Owen ed., *Studies in the Economic and Social History of Palestine in the Nineteenth and Twentieth Centuries* (Carbondale, Ill., 1982)

Derek Penslar, *Zionism and Technocracy: The Engineering of Jewish Settlement in Palestine, 1870–1918* (Bloomington, 1991)

Yehoshua Porath, *The Emergence of the Palestinian-Arab National Movement, 1918–1929* (London, 1974)

—— *The Palestine-Arab National Movement: From Riots to Rebellion, 1929–1939* (London, 1977)

Itamar Rabinovich, *The Road Not Taken: Early Arab–Israeli Negotiations* (New York, 1991)

Jehuda Reinharz, 'Old and New Yishuv: The Jewish Community in Palestine at the Turn of the Twentieth Century', *Jewish Studies Quarterly*, 1: 1 (September 1993), 54–71

Eugene L. Rogan and Avi Shlaim eds., *The War for Palestine: Rewriting the History of 1948* (Cambridge, 2001)

Yezid Sayigh, *Armed Struggle and the Search for State: The Palestinian National Movement, 1949–1993* (Oxford, 1997)

— 'The Palestinian Strategic Impasse', *Survival*, 44: 4 (Winter 2002–3), pp. 7–21.

Zeev Schiff and Ehud Ya'ari, *Israel's Lebanon War* (New York, 1984)

— *Intifada: The Palestinian Uprising – Israel's Third Front* (New York, 1990)

Alexander Schölch, 'The Demographic Development of Palestine, 1850–1882', *International Journal of Middle East Studies*, 17 (1985), 485–505

Enzo Sereni and R. E. Ashery eds., *Jews and Arabs in Palestine: Studies in a National and Colonial Problem* (New York, 1936)

Gershon Shafir, *Land, Labor and the Origins of the Israeli–Palestinian Conflict, 1882–1914* (Cambridge, 1989)

Gershon Shafir and Yoav Peled, *Being Israeli: The Dynamics of Multiple Citizenship* (Cambridge, 2002)

Anita Shapira, *Land and Power: The Zionist Resort to Force* (New York, 1992)

Greg Shapland, *Rivers of Discord: International Water Disputes in the Middle East* (New York, 1997)

Avi Shlaim, *Collusion Across the Jordan: King Abdullah, the Zionist Movement, and the Partition of Palestine* (New York, 1988)

— *The Iron Wall: Israel and the Arab World* (New York, 2000)

Barbara J. Smith, *The Roots of Separatism in Palestine: British Economic Policy, 1920–1929* (Syracuse, NY, 1993)

Arnon Soffer, *Rivers of Fire: The Conflict over Water in the Middle East* (Lanham, Md., 1999)

Ehud Sprinzak, *Brother Against Brother: Violence and Extremism in Israeli Politics from Altalena to the Rabin Assassination* (New York, 1999)

Kenneth W. Stein, *The Land Question in Palestine, 1917–1939* (Chapel Hill, 1984)

— 'Palestine's Rural Economy, 1917–1939', *Studies in Zionism*, 8: 1 (1987), 25–49

Bernard Wasserstein, *The British in Palestine: The Mandatory Government and the Arab–Jewish Conflict, 1917–1929* (2nd edn, Oxford, 1991)

— *Divided Jerusalem: The Struggle for the Holy City* (rev. edn, London, 2002)

World Bank, *Poverty in the West Bank and Gaza*, World Bank Report No. 22312-GZ, 18 June 2001

— *Fifteen Months – Intifada, Closures and Palestinian Economic Crisis: An Assessment*, 18 March 2002

Meir Yaish, 'Class Structure in a Deeply Divided Society: Class and Ethnic Inequality in Israel, 1974–1991', *British Journal of Sociology*, 52: 3 (Sept. 2001), 409–39

Elias Zureik, 'Constructing Palestine through Surveillance Practices', *British Journal of Middle Eastern Studies*, 28: 2 (2001), 205–27

INDEX

A

Abdullah I, King 102, 105, 182

Abu Dis 161

Acre: 107; sanjak of 103

Agmon, Lake 84

Ahad Ha'am (Asher Ginzberg) 11

Al-Ahram 28

Algeria 78

Allan, J. A. 88–90

Allon, Yigal 123–5

Almog, Oz 32, 34–5

Arab League 141, 181, 184

Arafat, Yasir 25, 102, 172–3, 185, 187–9, 189

Arava desert 81

Argentina 26–7

Ariel 135

Arlosoroff, Haim 14–15

Ashdod 145

Ashkenazim 34, 40–41, 43

B

Balfour, Lord 104

Balfour Declaration (1917) 11, 102–3, 106, 178–9

Bank of Israel 67, 68

Barak, Ehud 128, 145, 147, 155, 157, 161, 189–90

Barkai, Haim 39

Beduin 9, 15–16, 19

Beersheba 74

Begin, Menahem 34, 35, 38, 106, 122, 126, 186

Beirut, sanjak of 103

Beit Hanina 161

Beit Nuba 77

Ben-Eliezer, Binyamin 149

Ben Gurion, David 33, 109, 100, 183

Bennett, J. S. 22–3

Bethlehem 77, 163

Borokhov, Ber 31–2

Bourcart, Max 81

B'Tselem 134

France 104, 183
French, Lewis 52–4
Frishman, David 33
Frost, Robert 147

G
Gaza Strip: 24–6, 28, 57–65,
74, 78, 91, 141, 147,
168, 183, 184, 188
Jewish settlements in
60–61, 92, 130, 132-7,
144, 152–7
Germany 8, 15, 27, 39, 42
Gethsemane, Garden of 77
Ghana 67
Ginzburg, Yitzhak 165
Gipsies 9
Giv'at Ze'ev 161
Glasgow 117
Golan Heights 122, 125,
130, 184–5
Goldstein, Baruch 136, 188
Gorni, Yosef 110
Great Britain 183
Greece 78
Guri, Haim 33
Gush Emunim 125, 128,
130, 136
Gush Etzion 135

H
Ha'aretz 146, 170
Habad sect 165
Haifa: 79, 107, 111, 117–18,
179
oil refinery 39; University
of 27
Halutza dunes 145
Hamas movement 161, 168
Hatikva district (Tel Aviv) 67
Hauran district 103
Hebrew University of
Jerusalem 29, 42
Hebron 126, 134–6, 188,
189
Hedjaz 105
Herut Party 106
Herzl, Theodor 11, 74–6,
177–8
Herzliya 28
Histadrut 38
Hitler, Adolf 7, 180
Hizbollah organization 155
Hope-Simpson, Sir John
50–51, 54, 180
Huleh, Lake 81–4
Husayn, Sharif 102
Husayni, Hajj Amin al- 107,
168, 179

Hussein, King 125, 187, 189

I

India 99
Institute for Palestine Studies
10
intifada:
first (1987–93) 25, 62, 78,
187; second (2000–) 3,
62, 63–4, 78, 96–7, 130,
140–41, 147, 156, 172,
189
Iran 26, 99
Iraq 99, 187–8
Ireland 99
Islam 164–6
Israel:
1956 war 183; 1967 war
122, 184; 1973 war 185;
agriculture 59, 89–90;
Arabs in 23–6, 56–7,
167–9; army 154; birth
rates 26; borders
140–52; Central Bureau
of Statistics 69;
conversions 69, 130;
diamond industry 65;
economy 58–9, 62, 65,
89; emigration 27, 66;

environment 73–97;
Foreign Ministry 97;
forests 74–6, 78;
historiography 3, 35, 76,
110; immigration 7–8,
23, 25–7, 29, 40, 56, 66,
155; Knesset 27, 69,
166; labour 44, 56-7,
59–67, 71, 151; Labour
Party 45, 89–90, 128;
Law of Return 68;
Ministry of Interior 69,
70; Ministry of Labour
27, 60, 68; Ministry of
National Infrastructures
93; National Insurance
Institute 41; National
Security Council 139;
National Water Carrier
86; population 23–30;
population density 74;
poverty 60; public
opinion polls 141,
173–4; social divisions
40–43; Southern district
74; Supreme Court 70,
164; technology sector
65; tourist industry 61,
65; unemployment 65–6;

mandate (1920–48) 6,
8–9, 12–23, 79, 104,
114–18, 122, 163–4,
179–82; census (Turkish)
9 (1922) 15–16, 180
(1931) 16–21, 52, 180;
Christians 6, 20, 56;
citriculture 38, 46, 55;
economy 38–9, 45–6,
56, 58–60, 63–4, 151;
education 35, 38;
environment 73–97;
forests 74–8; human
rights 172; immigration
6-9, 12–16, 22, 25–6,
36, 38, 177–8; infant
mortality 20–21; Jewish
National Home in 11,
12, 122; Jews 6, 8, 15,
20–23, 31–45; labour
31, 39, 55, 59–67, 151;
land issue 19, 46–55,
109, 113; life expectancy
21; Muslims 6, 8, 20–21,
45, 47, 56; Ottoman 6,
8–11, 76, 99, 177–8;
partition proposals
107–14, 118–23, 169,
181; population 6, 8–30,

47, 109–10; public
opinion polls 172–3;
riots (1920) 179 (1921)
179 (1929) 50, 180
(1933) 180; Royal
Commission (1936–7)
22, 106–12, 181;
Southern District 15–16,
116; tourism 65;
urbanization 36–8, 45–6,
59, 116; water 78–97;
White Paper (1922) 180
(1939) 22, 181
Palestine Arab Executive 52
Palestine Broadcasting
Service 116–17
Palestine Land Development
Company 82
Palestine Liberation
Organization (PLO) 5,
122–5, 168, 184–5
Palestine National Covenant
122
Palestinian Arabs 1–4, 6,
8–10, 14–15, 18–26,
29–30, 139
labour 39, 59-67, 139-40,
147, 149-51; refugees
56, 57, 157–61